The Milford Series:
Popular Writers of Today
Volume Forty
ISSN 0163-2469

DEMON PRINCE

The Dissonant Worlds of Jack Vance

Jack Rawlins
California State University, Chico

BORGO PRESS / WILDSIDE PRESS

www.wildsidepress.com

CONTENTS

Abbreviations		3
Chronology		5
I.	About Jack Vance	9
II.	Vance's Worlds	12
III.	Vance's Words	49
IV.	Vance's Plots	66
V.	Afterword: New Directions	86
VI.	An Interview with Jack Vance	88
VII.	Selective Secondary Bibliography	97
Index		100

Library of Congress Cataloging in Publication Data:

Rawlins, Jack, 1946-
   Demon prince.

(Milford series : popular writers of today ; v. 40)
Bibliography: p.
   1. Vance, Jack, 1916-   —Criticism and interpretation. I. Title. II. Series.
PS3572.A424Z85   813'.54   81-21600
ISBN 0-89370-163-7
ISBN 0-89370-263-3

Copyright © 1986 by Jack Rawlins.
All rights reserved. No part of this book may be reproduced in any form without the expressed written consent of the publisher. Published by arrangement with the author. Printed in the United States of America by Van Volumes, Ltd., Wilbraham, MA.

Produced, designed, and published by R. Reginald and Mary A. Burgess, The Borgo Press, P.O. Box 2845, San Bernardino, CA 92406, USA. Cover design by Michael Pastucha.

First Edition——June, 1986

ABBREVIATIONS

A thread by itself is without meaning or worth.

The works cited in this book are listed below, in alphabetical order by abbreviation, with title, series number (where appropriate), and the specific edition used by the author. All are by Jack Vance unless otherwise indicated.

a	An anthology.
A	*The Anome* (Durdane #1). New York: Dell, 1971.
As	*The Asutra* (Durdane #3). New York: Ace, 1973.
BD	*The Book of Dreams* (Demon Prince #5). New York: DAW, 1981.
BFM	*The Brave Free Men* (Durdane #2). New York: Ace, 1972.
BJV	*The Best of Jack Vance.* New York: Pocket Books, 1976.
BP	*Big Planet.* New York: Ace, 1957.
BW	*The Blue World.* New York: Ballantine, 1966.
CC	*City of the Chasch* (Planet of Adventure #1). New York: Ace, 1968.
D	*The Dirdir* (Planet of Adventure #3). New York: Ace, 1969.
DE	*The Dying Earth.* New York: Hillman, 1950.
DM	*The Dragon Masters* (b/w *FGB*). New York: Ace, 1962.
DP	A Demon Prince novel.
E	*Emphyrio.* New York: Dell, 1969.
EFM	*Eight Fantasms and Magics.* New York: Macmillan, 1969.
EO	*The Eyes of the Overworld.* London: Mayflower, 1972.
F	*The Face* (Demon Prince #4). New York: DAW, 1979.
FGB	*The Five Gold Bands* (b/w *DM*). New York: Ace, 1963.
FT	*Future Tense.* New York: Ballantine, 1964.
GE	*The Galactic Effectuator.* San Francisco: Underwood/Miller, 1980.
GM	*Green Magic.* San Francisco: Underwood/Miller, 1979.
GP	*The Gray Prince.* New York: Avon, 1975.
HI	*The Houses of Iszm* (b/w *ST*). New York: Ace, 1964.
JV	Underwood, Tim, and Chuck Miller, eds. *Jack Vance,* New York: Taplinger Publishing Co., 1980.
KM	*The Killing Machine* (Demon Prince #2). New York: Berkley, 1964.
L	*Lyonesse.* New York: Berkley Books, 1983.
LC	*The Last Castle.* New York: Ace, 1966.
LM	*Lost Moons.* San Francisco: Underwood/Miller, 1982.
LP	*The Languages of Pao.* New York: Ace, 1958.
MA	*Marune: Alastor 993.* London: Coronet, 1978.
MM	"The Moon Moth," in *The Science Fiction Hall of Fame,* vol. IIB, ed. Ben Bova., New York: Doubleday, 1973.

MO   *Monsters in Orbit.* New York: Ace, 1965.
MR   A Magnus Ridolph story.
MT   *Maske: Thaery.* New York: Berkley, 1976.
MWMR *The Many Worlds of Magnus Ridolph.* New York: Ace, 1966.
P   *The Pnume* (Planet of Adventure #4). New York: Ace, 1970.
PA   A Planet of Adventure novel.
POL *The Palace of Love* (Demon Prince #3). New York: Berkley, 1967.
SO   *Space Opera.* New York: DAW, 1979.
SOK *Slaves of the Klau.* London: Coronet, 1980.
SOW *Servants of the Wankh* (Planet of Adventure #2). New York: Ace, 1969.
ST   *Son of the Tree* (b/w *HI*). New York: Ace, 1964.
StK *The Star King* (Demon Prince #1). New York: Berkley, 1964.
SW   *Showboat World.* London: Coronet, 1977.
T   *Trullion: Alastor 2262.* London: Mayflower, 1979.
TLF *To Live Forever.* New York: Ballantine, 1956.
TWS *Thrilling Wonder Stories* [magazine].
W   *Wyst: Alastor 1716.* New York: DAW, 1978.
WB   *The World Between and Other Stories.* New York: Ace, 1965.
WJV *The Worlds of Jack Vance.* New York: Ace, 1973.

CHRONOLOGY

Every aspect exaggerated, every quality dramatized.

Vance's work, like much of science fiction, is a maze of reprintings, rewritings, title changes, reeditings, fix-ups, anthologizing, and repackaging. I have not attempted to follow every turn, but have listed short stories by date for their first appearance in the magazines, and noted in parentheses afterwards their inclusion in collections of Vance's work. Books which include unrelated short stories have their contents entered separately in the chronology, by magazine publication; where books have been made up of interconnected tales or chronological episodes (such as *Dying Earth*, *Eyes of the Overworld*, *Cugel's Saga*), I have only entered the whole book. Novels that have been published in magazines are listed by book publication date, with magazine publication date in parentheses if different. Short stories are identified by the magazine in which they appeared, but not by issue number or date. Works are identified first by their earliest or most familiar title, whichever seems most helpful, with alternate titles in parentheses. Readers seeking more extensive information on Vance's publishing history should consult Levak and Underwood's bibliography, or Cockrum's unpublished masterpiece (see bibliography).

1945   "The World-Thinker" (*TWS*) (*LM*)

1946   "Phalid's Fate" (*TWS*); "Planet of the Black Dust" (*Startling*)

1947   "I'll Build Your Dream Castle" (*Astounding*) (*LM*)

1948   "Hard Luck Diggings"; "Sanatoris Short-Out" (*Startling*) (MR); "The Unspeakable McInch" (*Startling*) (*MWMR*)

1949   "The King of Thieves" (*Startling*) (*MWMR*) (*WJV*); "The Howling Bounders" (*Startling*) (*MWMR*); "The Sub-Standard Sardines" (*Startling*) (MR)

1950   "Cosmic Hotfoot" (aka "To B or Not to C or to D") (*Startling*) (MR); *The Dying Earth* (a series of related tales previously published separately); "New Bodies for Old" (*TWS*); "The Potters of Firsk" (*Astounding*) (*LM*); "The Spa of the Stars" (*Startling*) (*MWMR*) "Ultimate Quest" (*Super*

Science Stories)

1951 "Brain of the Galaxy" (later "The New Primes") (*Worlds Beyond*) (*EFM, WJV, WB*); "Dover Spargill's Ghastly Floater" (*Marvel SF*); "Golden Girl" (*Marvel SF*); "Masquerade on Dicantropus" (*Startling*); "Men of the Ten Books" (*Startling*); "Overlords of Maxus" (*TWS*); "The Plagian Siphon" (*TWS*); "Temple of Han" (*Planet Stories*); "Winner Lose All" (*Galaxy*) (LM)

1952 "Abercrombie Station" (*TWS*) (*BJV, MO*); "Cholwell's Chickens" (*TWS*) (*MO*); "The Kokod Warriors" (*TWS*) (*WJV, MWMR*); "Noise" (*Startling*) (*EFM*); "Planet of the Damned" (as *Slaves of the Klau*, 1958; later published as *Gold and Iron*); "Sabotage on the Sulphur Planet" (*Startling*) (*LM*); "Seven Exists from Bocz" (*The Rhodomagnetic Digest*) (*LM*); "Telek" (*Astounding*) (*EFM*)

1953 "DP!" (*Avon SF and F Reader*); "Ecological Onslaught" (later "The World Between") (*Future*) (*WJV, WB*); *The Space Pirate* (later *The Five Gold Bands*) (1950); "Four Hundred Blackbirds" (*Future*); "The Mitr" (*Vortex*) (*GM*); "Shape-Up" (*Cosmos SF*); "Sjambak" (*Worlds of If*); "Three-legged Joe" (*Startling*); *Vandals of the Void*

1954 "The Enchanted Princess" (later "The Dreamer") (*Orbit*); "When the Five Moons Rise" (*Cosmos SF*) (*EFM*)

1955 "The Devil on Salvation Bluff" (*Star SF Stories #3*) (*WJV, WB*); "Gift of Gab" (*Astounding*) (*FT*); "Meet Miss Universe" (*Fantastic Universe*) (*LM*)

1956 "The Phantom Milkman" (*Other Worlds*); *To Live Forever*; "Where Hesperus Falls" (*Fantastic Universe*)

1957 *Big Planet* (1952); "House Lords" (*Saturn*); "The Men Return" (*Infinity*) (*EFM, WJV, WB, GM*); "A Practical Man's Guide" (*Space SF Mag*); *Take My Face* (by "Peter Held") [mystery]; *Isle of Peril* (by "Alan Wade") [mystery]

1958 "Coup de Grace" (orig. "Worlds of Origin") (*Super SF*) (*MWMR, WJV*); *Languages of Pao* (1957); "The Miracle Workers" (*Astounding*) (*EFM, GM*); "Parapsyche" (*Amazing*); "Ullward's Retreat" (*Galaxy*) (*BJV, GM*)

1959 *Dodkin's Job* (*Amazing*) (*FT*)

1960 *The Man in the Cage* [mystery]

1961 "I-C-A-BEM" (later "Augmented Agent") (*Amazing*); "The Moon Moth" (*Galaxy*) (*BJV, WJV, WB, GM*)

1962 "Sail 25" (orig. "Gateway to Strangeness" *(Amazing)* *(FT, BJV)*

1963 *The Dragon Masters* (1962); "Green Magic" *(F and SF)* *(GM)*

1964 *Future Tense* (later *Dust of Far Suns*) (a); *The Houses of Iszm* (1954); *The Killing Machine* (DP #2); *Son of the Tree* (1951); *The Star King* (DP #1) (1963)

1965 "Alfred's Ark" *(New Worlds)*; *Space Opera; Monsters in Orbit* (a); *The World Between and Other Stories* (aka *The Moon Moth and Other Stories*); *A Room To Die In* (as "Ellery Queen") [mystery]

1966 *The Blue World* (1964); *The Brains of Earth; The Eyes of the Overworld* (Seven related episodes previously published separately) (1965); *The Many Worlds of Magnus Ridolph* (a); "The Secret" *(Impulse)* *(GM)*; *The Madman Theory* (as "Ellery Queen") [mystery]; *The Fox Valley Murders* [mystery]

1967 *The Last Castle* (1966) *(BJV)*; "The Man From Zodiac" *(Amazing)*; "The Narrow Land" *(Fantastic)* *(GM)* (Published as a book in 1982); *The Palace of Love* (DP #3) (1966); *The Pleasant Grove Murders* [mystery]

1968 *City of the Chasch* (also called *Chasch*) (PA #1); "Sulwen's Planet" *(The Farthest Reaches*, edited by Joseph Elder)

1969 *The Dirdir* (PA #3); *Eight Fantasms and Magics* (also published as *Fantasms and Magics*) (a); *Emphyrio; Servants of the Wankh* (PA #2); *The Deadly Isles* [mystery]

1970 *The Pnume* (PA #4)

1973 *The Anome* (orig. *The Faceless Man*) (Durdane #1) (1971); *The Brave Free Men* (Durdane #2) (1972); "Morreion" *(Flashing Swords #1)* (Reprinted in *Rialto the Marvellous*, 1984); "Rumfuddle" *(Three Trips in Time and Space*, edited by Robert Silverberg) *(BJV)*; *Trullion: Alastor 2262; The Worlds of Jack Vance* (a); *Bad Ronald* [mystery]

1974 "Assault on a City" *(Universe 4*, edited by Terry Carr) *(LM)*; *The Asutra* (Durdane #3) (1973); *The Gray Prince* (orig. *The Domains of Koryphon*)

1975 "The Dogtown Tourist Agency" *(Epoch)* *(GE)*; *Marune: Alastor 993; Showboat World* (also published as *The Magnificent Showboats of the Lower Vissel River, Lune XXIII South, Big Planet* [the original title]); *The Moon Moth and Other Stories* (a)

1976   *Maske: Thaery*; *The Best of Jack Vance* (a)

1977   "Freitzke's Turn"   (*Triax*, edited by Robert Silverberg) (*GE*)

1978   *Wyst: Alastor 1716*

1979   *The Face* (DP #4); *Green Magic* (a); *The View from Chickweed's Window* [mystery]; *The House on Lily Street* [mystery]; *The Seventeen Virgins* (story); *Morreion: A Tale of the Dying Earth* (story); *The Bagful of Dreams* [story]

1980   *Galactic Effectuator* (a reprint of two related tales); *Nopalgarth* (a reprinting in one volume of the three novels: *The Brains of Earth*, *Son of the Tree*, and *The Houses of Iszm*)

1981   *The Book of Dreams* (DP #5)

1982   *Lost Moons* (a); *The Narrow Land* (a)

1983   *Cugel's Saga* (a series of episodes previously published separately); *Lyonesse* (also called *Lyonesse, Book I: Suldrun's Garden*)

1984   *Rhialto the Marvellous* (a reprint of "Morreion" and two new stories of the Dying Earth); *The Complete Magnus Ridolph* (a); *Cugel's Saga*

1985   *The Green Pearl* (also called *Lyonesse: The Green Pearl*); *Light from a Lone Star* (a)

Vance also wrote six teleplays for the *Captain Video* TV series in 1952 and 1953.

Two of Vance's mystery stories (written as John Holbrook Vance) have been turned into TV productions: "Bad Ronald" (ABC *Wednesday Night Movie of the Week*, 1974) and "The Man in the Cage" (*Thriller*, NBC, Jan. 17, 1961).

I
ABOUT JACK VANCE

Had I followed an early bent,
I might have been a great scientist.

Jack Vance has always been reluctant to divulge much about his life, not because there's anything to hide, but because, he says, it doesn't interest him to do so. He's a friendly but not public person who would prefer that his books speak for themselves. As a result, he has become surrounded with an almost inexplicable aura of anonymity and reclusiveness—so much so that for many years a persistent rumor circulated within the library community that Vance was in fact a pen name for Henry Kuttner.
He is, in actuality, a remarkably normal person whose life centers around his work, his house, his wife Norma, and his son John II. The family gardens, sails, and cooks together. His life has been remarkably stable: he's been living in and working on the same house for thirty years, he and Norma have been married nearly forty years (married August 1946), and he has devoted himself to the same career—freelance fiction—for the same four decades.
Jack was born John Holbrook Vance (the *nom de plume* on his mystery and detective fiction) in San Francisco, California, on August 28, 1920, a date some critics believe is at least four years too late. His great-great-grandfather supposedly arrived in California eleven years before the Gold Rush. Vance grew up in the country around the Sacramento River delta. He has said that as a youth he would stand by the mailbox waiting for the latest issue of *Weird Tales*, and it has been argued that his work was heavily influenced by the style and tone of that magazine. He seems to have spent his early years reading the popular pulp adventure fiction of the day—Robert E. Howard, Edgar Rice Burroughs, the Oz books, Clark Ashton Smith.
He graduated from high school early, worked for a few years, then entered the University of California, Berkeley, majoring in mining engineering. He soon moved to physics, journalism, and perhaps English (Norma says he "took a little of everything"), graduating with a B.A. in 1942. During the rest of the war years he served as a merchant seaman, and later worked as a carpenter and a horn player in jazz bands.
Toward the end of his college days he decided to become a freelance writer. He has always resisted the temptation to attribute his art to the direct influence of other writers or works, claiming that he learned the craft of writing by doing

vast amounts of it during a long, solitary apprenticeship in the forties and early Fifties. He discounts much of his early work as the hasty first drafts of an unpolished tyro.

His first real success came with the Magnus Ridolph stories, featuring a cocky little dandy who trouble-shoots intergalactic problems with the Vancean hero's mixture of logic, wry self-interest, and con artistry. In 1950 Vance published his first novel, *The Dying Earth*, a series of related tales he had written in previous years and been unable to sell separately. Considered by many a masterpiece of fantasy adventure, the book is set in an infinitely distant future when the sun is burning down and the world is dying with it, the few survivors bathed in ennui. It demonstrates for the first time Vance's ability to capture subtle, evocative, emotively-rich ambiances on paper.

In 1963 he published *The Dragon Masters*, set on an alien world where man's descendants wage war with an off-world race of dragonoid aliens, each side using troops of geneticallyengineered mutants bred from captured enemy soldiers. The book won a Hugo Award for short fiction from the World Science Fiction Convention. In 1963 he also published *The Star King*, the first of five novels centered on the Demon Princes. These books constitute his finest, most sustained series of novels, as well as his best developed character, Kirth Gersen. Gersen's quest to rid the galaxy of its five worst outlaws (one per novel), becomes a distinct kind of nightmare, with each book suffused by its own distinct flavor, exquisite and elusive.

In 1965 Vance published *The Eyes of the Overworld*, often called a sequel to *The Dying Earth*, but in reality a completely different book. Whereas *The Dying Earth* is melancholic, brooding, mythic, full of grand gesture and stately allegory, *The Eyes of the Overworld* is devoted to the black-comic adventures of Vance's great con artist, Cugel the Clever, who wanders through a world populated entirely by other con artists, with each new encounter a battle to see who out-cons whom.

1966 brought *The Last Castle*, a novella that won both the Nebula Award from the Science Fiction Writers of America and the Hugo. This curious story features a noble class who reside, fastidious and effete, as self-imposed prisoners in their own splendidly archaic castles, while a race of downtrodden country-dwellers methodically destroy one fastness after another. 1968 saw *City of the Chasch*, the first of four volumes in the Planet of Adventure series, the most sophisticated expression of a myth first used in *Big Planet*, in which a culturally neutral Earthman wanders through a series of small cultural enclaves, constantly facing anew the challenge of decoding and surviving a fresh set of cultural mores and shibboleths. In 1969 he published *Emphyrio*, the best expression of another Vancean myth, in which an unremarkable but fey youth meanders though life gnawed by unresolved questions. His quest for answers almost accidentally topples a stagnant, repressive social structure.

In 1975 Vance received the Jupiter Award for best novelette of the year from the Instructors of Science Fiction in Higher

Education, for "The Seventeen Virgins" (later reprinted as an episode in *Cugel's Saga*). He has also been Guest of Honor at science fiction conventions in Sweden (1976), Vancouver (1979), and Melbourne. In 1984 he was voted a Life Achievement Award at the World Fantasy Convention. Vance has also carved out a small reputation as a mystery novelist, winning an Edgar Award in 1960 for *The Man in the Cage*.

A well-travelled man, Vance has spent much of the last thirty years building a quirky, idiosyncratic house set on a steep hillside deep in the eucalyptus groves of the Oakland hills, with hand-made Italian oak panelled ceiling in the dining room, among other novelties. He says that whenever the house is finished, he'll start remodelling. His hobbies include classical jazz, bluewater sailing, and carpentry.

Vance talks about his work as something quite apart from the science-fiction mainstream, as he himself stays aloof from the rather inbred SF community. He reads little science fiction, his friends in the business (like Frank Herbert and Poul Anderson) are staunch but select, and he almost never makes public appearances at conventions. When I asked him if he had seen any recent science-fiction, he said only *Star Wars*, because the producers had sent him free tickets. He takes a fierce pride in his work and very much wants it to be considered seriously, but has little interest in formal critical attention or attendant honors: when I asked him about the numerous awards he'd received, he couldn't remember the name of the World Fantasy Convention plaque which he had received only months earlier, and could not recall his Jupiter Award at all.

He knows his own work well, has the names of characters and plot details from twenty-five-year-old stories at his fingertips, but is obviously uncomfortable discussing his work as ideology or implied lesson; he thinks of himself as a writer of adventure stories, and is comfortable talking about his art in dramatic terms—plotting, pacing, characterization, dramatic timing, and the like. His reluctance to support an ideology is also true of his private life as well: he has officially described his personal politics as "above and between left and right," and his religion affiliation as "none."

—Jack Rawlins
Chico, California
November, 1985

II
VANCE'S WORLDS

*A Treasure of Spectacular Devices
for Diversion and Thrill and Catharsis*

Vance's worlds are over-stuffed, struggling to contain more alien cultures, flora, colors, and smells than the page can hold. Furniture spills forth from the pages, like bric-a-brac in the home of an inveterate antique collector. A world Alfred Bester would spend a novel sculpting, or a more thrifty writer would milk for a series, Vance strikes off in one dazzling blow, and is soon bounding off to another, never to return. From melange, *Dune*'s prescient spice, Frank Herbert made six volumes and thousands of pages of text; from charnay, the fruit of ecstasy and death in *The Book of Dreams*, an equally pregnant symbol, Vance makes one page and a single short plot episode (*BD*, 65).

It is central to Vance's art that more is thrown away than kept. Always we catch glimpses of the infinite riches that lurk just outside our vision. In *The Killing Machine*, Gersen goes to Thamber, the home of Alusz Iphegenia and Kokkor Hekkus. There he experiences many wonders, but finally asks Iphegenia, "What of the rest of the planet?" A torrent follows:

> Everywhere it is different. In Birzul, the Godmus keeps a harem of ten thousand concubines. Every day he enlists ten maidens and discharges ten, or if he happens to be in a bad humor drowns them. In Calastang, the Divine Eye rides through the city carried on a vermilion altar forty yards long and forty yards high. The Lathcar Gentry keep racing-men—slave runners especially bred and trained for the Lath Race Meets... (*KM*, 115).

And the passage goes on, a monument to Vance's prodigality of imagination. Similarly, in *The Eyes of the Overworld* Cugel asks if there is not an alternate route, and a paragraph delineates the wonders he would have encountered if he had happened to go the other way (*EO*, 65).

Vance is best known for creating eccentric cultures, and the Tschai tetralogy is a good example of the almost wasteful extravagance he employs. Tschai is so rich with peoples that the protagonist Adam Reith cannot hope to make contact with all in four volumes of hectic traveling. The planet knows five major races: the Chasch, the Wankh, the Dirdir, the Pnume, and Man.

Each of the first four has bred men in its own image to serve it, and these men have become physically and psychically something between Man and their masters: the Chaschmen, Wankhmen, Dirdirmen, and Pnumekin. The Chasch also come in racial varieties, each physically and psychologically distinct: the Old Chasch, Blue Chasch, and Green Chasch. The men of Tschai live in countless cultural enclaves, from the hypersophisticated Yao of Cath to the commercial societies of shipping and trade—the schizophrenic Blacks and Purples of Ao Hiddis; the industrious Lokhars, the methodically untrustworthy Thangs—to the wild tribes of the savage outback—the Kruthe, who wear ancestral emblems and derive their tribal personalities from them, the Khors with their forest sex rites, the Ilanth, the master scouts. In addition the planet is well-populated with beasts of varying degrees of intelligence, from the mad, man-like Phung to the dread Berl. Reith lives among some of these for a time; others we merely observe from a distance, and still others we only catch hints of. Vance has done more than think up bizarrely alien names; each sentient race has its own psychology and its own distinct symbolic furniture—dress, architecture, religion, pecking order—that is the physical expression of that unique cultural psyche.

In Vance's world, each item in the universe exhales a unique emotive aura. Sailmaker Beach "resemble[s] no other locale in the known universe" (*StK*, 113), and everything else shares this quality. Gersen seeks information at a Sandusker victual shop and is encouraged to try the food by the young Sandusker running the place:

> The youth went to one of the tubs, dipped up a wad of glistening, black-encrusted maroon paste. "Taste! Judge for yourself..."
> Gersen gave a fatalistic shrug, tasted...
> "Well?" asked the youth.
> "If anything," said Gersen at last, "it tastes worse than it smells."
> The youth sighed. "Such is the general consensus" (*KM*, 25).

The taste is unique, indescribable, intensely, and unapologetically what it is—the quality most prized in Vance's world. The Sanduskers are as distinct in their psychology as in their cuisine: the youth addresses Gersen in "a complex mood of many discords: sad pride, whimsical malice, insolent humility" (*KM*, 24). Vance searches for the right vortex of adjectives to capture the nameless flavor, in a world where each flavor is idiosyncratic and the flavors are without end.

The parade of idiosyncratic cultures never ends: the Byzantaurs of Sirius, of whom it is said "there are three sex processes, and each of the 'zants' is capable of performing two of them," so communication between human and "zant" is prone to "an untold number of misunderstandings" (*SO*, 53); the Calbyssinians of *Klau*, to whom a person's sex is his most carefully guarded secret, and who consequently devote all their energies to trying to tease and trick the secret out of each other (*K*, 52); the Funambulous Evangels, who spend their lives on tightropes to avoid trampling the dust of dead men (*EO*, 110); the Fwai-chi of Marune, whose reproductive hormones are in their skin, and who reproduce by nibbling each other, gestating the resultant bud on the wall of their stomachs, and vomiting the child into the world (*MA*, 38); the city of Zaccare, where each personal act must be accompanied by the appropriate personal scent, and designated odors exist for "the ensorcelment of a strange maiden," "to hint at revulsion," "at water-tasting" (one for morning, one for twilight), "to celebrate a murder," and so on (*KM*, 131); the Alula, whose girls wear precariously tilted caps, and who believe that caps are intimate apparel and that anyone who rights the cap must wed the violated maiden (*As*, 96); the Lokhars of Tschai, who bind themselves together with unshakable oaths sealed by twisting together hairs from each swearer's head, lighting the twist, and all inhaling the smoke (*SOW*, 130).

Often Vance's plots are little more than set-ups to justify a protagonist's flight through a series of such portraits, quickly struck off and juxtaposed in harsh dissonance—as when Etzwane of Durdane, in an attempt to muster a militia to combat the invading Rogushkoi, sets out to tour the cantons (counties) of Shant, to make sure that each is instating the draft according to his directives. Each paragraph is a new encounter with a different mindset: Etzwane must one moment deal with the Aglustids of Burazhesq Canton, who are such rabid conservationalists that they consider it murder to eat a fruit and rob a seed of its chance for life, and in the next moment with their next-door neighbors, the Shker of Shker Canton, who worship wickedness in the form of a pantheon of demons called the Golse (*BFM*, 60). In both cases, Etzwane's "dealings" amount to a brief portrait of the culture, a despairing shake of the head at the impossibility of communication, and on the next canton. At such times, Vance's world takes on the tempo and depth of a friend's hasty showing of the slides from his ten-day tour of Europe.

VANCE'S EXPOSITION

*As if the Abbatram of Pamfile were to
be liquified for smelling too strongly.*

Every SF writer faces the problem of exposition: how to educate the reader about the alien world he has just entered. Each SF reading experience begins with the fundamental questions: Where am I? What's going on? What are the laws of this new universe? Some writers simply tell us, by means of an omniscient narrator who speaks directly to us. This is no fun. The SF of the Campbell era is often maligned for using a weakly disguised form of this exposition, in which a conveniently ignorant and curious newcomer enters the scene at the beginning of the story and says, "I'm new here—fill me in on what's going on." Asimov is particularly dependent on this crutch, "Nightfall" being one example.

Vance, when he's good, refuses to help us so directly; he lets the representatives of each alien culture speak to each other, and allows the parameters of the new environment to become apparent to us by showing people unselfconsciously living by them. At its best, this method is like overhearing a fragment of conversation in the next aisle at the grocery store: a few words reveal an entire relationship, a value system, a worldview, in an epiphany which needs no narrator to interpret for us. For instance, when Adam Reith reaches Cath, where, we have been told, the hypersophisticated population suffers from *awaile*, fits of terminal despair, he takes a cab, and the driver in a few lines reveals everything there is to know about Cath. Reith sees a "morbidly suggestive" outdoor theatre and asks what it is. The driver replies:

> "The Circle, site of Pathetic Communion, as you can see. You are a stranger in Settra?"
> "Yes."
> The driver consulted a yellow cardboard schedule. "The next event is Ivensday, when a nineteen-score comes to clarify his horrible desperation. Nineteen! The most since the twenty-two of Agate Crystal's Lord Wis."
> "You mean he killed nineteen?"
> "Of course; what else? Four were children, but still a feat these days when folk are wary of *awaile*. All Settra will come to the expiation. If you're still in town you could hardly do more for your own soul's profit" (*SOW*, 69).

Reith responds with a noncommittal "Probably so," and we are left to construct the society implicit in the details: the schedule of executions always close to hand, the easy omission of the fact of murder in the slang "nineteen-score," the discounting of the four children (because killing children is too easy, we assume), the driver's pride in the killer's high score, the assumption that spiritual gain is to be had from the experience, the implication that the community is assisting the torture victim by "clarifying his desperation," thus helping him publish his personal Statement.

Vance's worlds *emerge*—and understanding dawns on us—as we experience these places like foreign visitors without benefit of a tour guide. When Etzwane and Ifness enter Shillinsk, the innkeeper mentions that he got his maimed leg by the hand of his mother, who did it to discourage the slave-takers (*As*, 46), and we understand the culture we have entered with an emotional immediacy no cultural anthropologist's lecture could match.

Vance delights in giving hints so slight that we can only catch a trace of the alien odor. When Apollon Zamp reminds the

15

crew of his showboat that the last time they played Port Fitz there was "some small trouble in connection with a lady wearing antlers," and concludes, "I don't care to desecrate another of their totems"—the mind is left to wonder (*ShW*, 14). And so with the careless seaman who patronized shops of both Blacks and Purples at Ao Hiddis, and "staggered aboard the ship with foam coming from his nose" (*SOW*, 60). When a Sarkoy Venefice is condemned to death for selling poison, a Rigellian newspaper comments that this is as ironical "as if the Abbatram of Pamfile were to be liquified for smelling too strongly" (*POL*, 6), and this is all we ever hear of the Abbatram and his culture. Liquified? Vance always strives to make the implications a notch more provocative.

In the Demon Prince series, Vance uses a narrative device that perfectly suits his expositional tastes: he begins each chapter with quotations from various sources within the fictional world—textbooks, manuals, monographs, histories, gospels, ancient scrolls, conversations, old saws, speeches, news commentary, interviews, poems, fables, slick magazine articles, and so on. The substance of the quotations usually bears on the plot at hand, but not necessarily: in the midst of *The Book of Dreams*, Vance quotes a passage from *Fauna of the Vegan Worlds*, Vol. III: *The Fish of Aloysius*, by Rapunzel K. Funk, on the Nighttrain, a fish that "peregrinates" from one point in the ocean to another, then turns around and returns to its starting point, over and over, for its entire life (*BD*, 57)—delightful, but entirely irrelevant to the novel.

The introductory quotations are a perfect vehicle for Vance to remove himself completely and allow us to see his worlds from points of view within the worlds themselves. They also make it impossible to see the world from a single controlling perspective: instead of "the author" directing our responses to the Institute, we see it through the eyes of representatives of many perspectives within the imagined world. Chapter 8 of *The Star King*, for instance, quotes from the television address by Madian Carbuke, Centennial of the Institute, of December 2, 1502, on the Institute's image of itself; quotes a short, cryptic dialogue between two Centennials about a third obnoxious colleague; and quotes the mottoes of the Institute ("A little knowledge is a dangerous thing; a great deal of knowledge is disaster"), and a popular paraphrase ("Someone else's ignorance is bliss"). The Institute is never "explained" to us in the usual way, but from such signs of its functioning in the world we construct a sense of what it is, the way a paleontologist constructs a Jurassic beast from footprints and fumets.

The best example of Vance's determination to deny us a single, objective, outside perspective on his creations, is the Baron Bodissey, the author of the frequently-quoted, interminable treatise on everything entitled *Life*. The Baron's work allows Vance to publish his most self-indulgent philosophical puffery, on questions we would all like to pretend to be experts on: What is life? What is the nature of Goodness? Why is there air?

Vance quotes *Life* several times, then offers us a fictional commentary on the Baron's fictional commentary—he quotes six reviews of *Life*, each more scathing than the last, each a parody of reviewing style ("A monumental work if you like monuments" begins the first) (*KM*, 118).

The introductory quotations also allow Vance to invent and experiment copiously with concepts and styles free of obligations to any larger structure. Here Vance can write in five different voices, in five different literary forms, representing five different races, on five different topics, in a page. Free from plot, Vance need never explain how he got there, and he need never stay. He can write a paragraph as the pompous pedant Calvin V. Calvert in *The Moral Essense of Civilization*, a sentence from a high-school textbook called *Human Institutions*, a short fable from the cryptic *Scroll From the Ninth Dimension*, tell a joke from the next planet en route, write a delightfully awful poem by the mad egomaniacal poet Navarth, and so on forever, without having to live with the consequences of any of it.

THE PRIMACY OF BACKGROUND

The unseen ghosts which never dissipate.

The furniture of Vance's world—the flora and fauna, the dress, the architecture, the sensual details of color and smell —*matters*, not as a support system for "story," as in conventional literary priorities, but as ends in themselves. In Vance, priorities often seem reversed—the "story" seems little more than a vehicle for the parade of alien furniture. We rush through the plot to get to the next meal lovingly detailed, the list of book titles in an alien library, the rules of the local field sport. To read past these things merely to get on with the story is to skip the heart of the work.

Vance instructs us in the new priorities with a personal convention: in many of his novels, the linear protagonist takes a long journey by air, cart, or boat across huge, trackless expanses. The journey frees him from the duties of plot, confines him to a small vessel, and idles him, so he has nothing to do but observe the details of landscape and savor the aura it projects. At such times, the furniture holds center stage, and we are asked to immerse ourselves in the alien texture. In Reith's flight by aircar across the Dead Steppe in *Wankh*, Gersen's voyage to the Palace of Love, and Etzwane's flight by air to Shillinsk (*As*, 30-43), the hero is typically lost and his vehicle frail, so that he must simply let the voyage happen to him and experience the experience, a symphony of sensual impacts, evocative alien names, and resonant colors.

At such times, there is always a lot of musing about important issues: one's youth, the future, racial history, death, loneliness. Typically, when Ifness and Etzwane camp for the night in the midst of their journey, they sense that even the blackness of the night is pungent with import:

> [Ifness] stood peering through the dark. "According to Kreposkin, yonder along the beach is the site of Suserane, a town built by the Shelm Fyrids some six thousand years ago...Caraz, then as now, was savage and vast. No matter how many enemies fell in battle, more always came..." (*As*, 35).

The rich resonance exhaled by such experience is so special that Vance makes up a word for it. Ifness says that all that remains of Suserane is *esmeric*, which he defines: "It derives from a dialect of old Caraz and means the association or atmosphere clinging to a place: the unseen ghosts, the dissipated sounds, the suffused glory, music, tragedy, exultation, grief, and terror, which never dissipates." Vance's heroes usually have a moment of insight when they realize that the plot is only something to be doing, while the important business of letting the furniture of the world infuse its esmeric into our souls goes on. Whether Etzwane finally discovers the secret of the Rogushkoi matters little; what *does* matter is that Etzwane will always be richer for having been exposed to the six-thousand-year-old city of Suserane, where "no matter how many enemies fell,...more always came," until the city was no more.

PURSUING THE SUBTLE ESMERIC

The emotion has no name,
but it is as rich as blood.

Vance loves to dramatize scenes of impossibly subtle, utterly alien, supremely imaginative esmerics, and to deliver. For example, *The Palace of Love* is based on such a promise: somewhere exists the legendary Palace of Love, pleasure dome of supreme sybarite Viole Falusche, where the limits of human pleasure are tested. In the end, we know, Gersen will get there, and Vance will have to duplicate Falusche's feat and create the Palace for us. Emotional intensity is easy to promise and hard to deliver; the ultimate meal, the ultimate horror, the most divine music, all usually fail to live up to advance billing. How successful is Vance? In the case of the Palace, not very, and Gersen and Falusche feel called upon to discuss the failure (*POL*, 168). There are some other places in which promised wonder fails to match our expectations; but usually Vance is successful beyond our hopes at giving life to the unimaginably beautiful, horrible, alien—and his success is amazing, because he dares to promise us anything, and then renders it in voluminous detail, as if Ridley Scott, the director of *Alien*, would invite the audience to come into the screen and scrutinize the alien up close. Vance's fiction is full of such triumphs: the social intercourse of the Sirenese in "Moon Moth"; the imagist competition in "The New Prime," where the most imaginative minds in the galaxy meet to produce the grandest mental images, with Vance describing the work of each contestant at length; the music of Dystar, the legendary minstrel, in Durdane; the supernal playing of the damned flautist met by Guyal of Sfere in *The Dying Earth*; the sculpture of Pharesm the Sorceror, product of five hundred years of exacting craftsmanship by a race of workmen bred solely for the project (*EO*); the non-causal phenomena of "The Men Return"; and so on.

Vance flaunts his genius by routinely describing masterworks of alien art. Consider what he undertakes in delineating Dystar's music or one of Apollon Zamp's fantasmagorical showboat performances: first, he must describe esthetic experience in prose, a difficult task at best; second, he promises that the experience will be matchless, unforgettable, overwhelming; third, he must overcome the SF albatross of alien verisimilitude—the work of art must follow *un*earthly logic and form, so that it strikes us as utterly new, yet it must also be convincing and compelling to our human sensibilities on first meeting. Dystar must play music like we've never heard, but we must instantly respond to the newness with affirmation: "Yes, this is splendid music." No other writer in SF asks so much of himself in this way.

On the other hand, despite Vance's matchless ability to realize the details of the alien surface and his prodigality of imagination, his career moves away from crowded canvasses toward landscapes of pregnant absences and esmerics so subtle and alien they cannot be described. When Jantiff of Wyst is setting out on the wilderness road, he is advised to build "four blazing fires against the gaunch" every night. "What is a gaunch?" he asks. "That question is often asked but never answered," is the laconic reply (*W*, 140). The gaunch never appears, so we never know what one is. As Vance's career continues, more and more of his work shares this characteristic of the gaunch—that we respond to it in terms of its absence or its incomprehensibility. In *The Gray Prince*, the urban Glissam visits the wild sarai, the steppes of the Alouan, and is deeply touched by the esmeric of the place; but in the midst of a long passage in which Vance tries to tell us what is evoking the primal response in Glissam, Vance says, "There was nothing to be seen..." (*GP*, 98). Most of Vance's recent work is like this: there is less and less furniture to see, and what *is* visible is less and less pyrotechnical. But the esmeric emerging from the minimalist landscape gets richer in ways Vance consistently refuses to verbalize. As Akadie of Trullion says about the climax of a hussade match, "The emotion has no name, but it is as rich as blood" (*T*, 182).

In one sense, this is only Vance's attempt to convince us that his music is even grander than our ears tell us it is, but in other terms it is at the center of a career-long movement toward the creation of an imagined world that is esmeric alone, free both of furniture and of a human perspective, in which the alien aura fills the nostrils without mediation. Vance's closest approximation to this ideal is *The Pnume*, the conclusion to the Tschai tetralogy. For three volumes the Pnume have loomed in the dark corners of Tschai, an incomprehensible terror lurking in underground passageways and dragging careless surface folk down to unguessable fates. Reith asks about them, and is told only, "When something terrible happens, it is safe to assume that the Pnume have been at work" (*CC*, 48).

Finally, our expectations are fulfilled; Reith is snatched by the Pnume and spends the bulk of the novel prowling their underground world. And what are the Pnume? What do they do? We never really know, because Reith can't comprehend what he sees. His first glimpse of the new world reveals the problem: "The passage opened into a cavern of almost purposeful roughness—or perhaps the rudeness concealed a delicacy beyond Reith's understanding" (*P*, 19). So it goes: Reith observes the Pnume doing incomprehensible things for incomprehensible purposes with incomprehensible artifacts—a series of curious pedestals, for instance, "the function of which Reith [can] not calculate" (*P*, 40). He meets a Pnumekin, Zap 210, whose face registers "expression[s] to which he [can] put no name" (*P*, 61). The Pnume landscape consists of next to nothing: rock tunnels, sterile rooms, silent figures in black cloaks—a world of black and grey. Yet we are constantly assured that there is a world of subtle intensity here, an intensity we are simply deaf to: the language is rich with untranslatable nuances (*P*, 40), Zap 210, for example, senses minute personality traits distinguishing the zombie Pnumekin from each other (*P*, 57).

This sounds boring, but it isn't, because it's exactly what Vance's world is all about. The world of the Pnume is in this sense the ultimate Vancean landscape, stripped of all furniture, all individual personality, all dramatic interest, so that the seven-million-year-old Pnume esmeric can impinge on us directly. Vance is often called the Father of Dungeons and Dragons by gameplayers who don't know his work very well, and the title certainly captures much of the spirit of his early work, overstuffed as it is with engines of fantasy, hardware, and dramatic encounter; but Vance moves away from this clutter, to worlds like Emphyrio's Amboy and Glinnes' Trullion, where little happens and the important things emerge through a static, bland surface. If *The Pnume* were a game, the object would be to sit still and try to sniff the alien odor of the corridors.

VANCE'S LOGISTICS

Space is foam.

Critics usually begin discussions of Vance by praising the depth and completeness of his imaginary worlds, his characters, and his social systems (see for example *JV* pp. 11, 19, 31, and 76 for four critics' statements of the truism). Yet this completeness is an illusion, and in fact is only a complexity of surface. In literal terms, Vance's worlds aren't real at all.

David Gerrold, in a review of *The Empire Strikes Back* in *Starlog* (#38, Sept. 1980), condemns the film as pleasant fluff, and finds the starslug sequence, in which the *Millennium Falcon* escapes from the bowel of a giant asteroidal worm, symptomatic of the film's shallowness. Sure, he says, the starslug is striking to the eye—but what does the thing eat? Lucas has failed to work out the logistics of keeping his striking creation alive.

SF has traditionally cared enormously about this kind of verisimilitude, and there is a kind of art where nothing is more important than Gerrold's kind of question: Heinlein's *The Moon Is a Harsh Mistress*, for example, where the logistics of social revolution and Darwinian social order in the lunar colony are essential to the validity of his statement. But to another kind of art—Vance's and Lucas's—such considerations are irrelevant; attempts to provide logistical machinery to justify the fantasy surfaces—explanations of what the starslug eats, how Darth Vader got his asthma, how the Demon Princes administer their empires of crime—are silly and usually destructive.

Vance's genius, like Dickens', lies in his ability to bring all of his meaning to the surface, so that his worlds project a dense mosaic of deeply-felt symbols. But to mistake that richness of facade with psychological or sociological realism is to court disaster. Vance does exactly this when his protagonists stay too long in one place and he is forced to flesh out the symbols. For instance, the Institute is a wonderful concept, but the closer we get to it the more incomplete it appears. When we are reading the introductory quotations and indirect references, the Institute seems awesome and profound; when Gersen visits a Ninety-Fourth Degree Fellow briefly in *The Killing Machine* (39), a bit of the wonder vanishes; in *The Book of Dreams*, the plot centers around the internal politics of the Institute, which now seems silly and unconvincing, like a Disneyland ride viewed from the wrong side. Such is the nature of fantasy abstractions—you can't follow them home and see how they live away from the set.

Vance's worlds *don't work*—his handling of space travel, for example. Every SF writer decides how literally he wants to handle the business of getting from one planet to another: innoculations, immunological checks, and quarantines; physical training to adjust to new gravities; chemical treatments for high-G acceleration; etc.—Or just walking off the ship and commenting on the puce sky. Vance is nearer the latter end of the spectrum. He gives occasional lip service to "equalizing atmospheres" and adjusting to local accents (*KM*, 88; *BD*, 22), but these are *pro forma*; in his world all planets are perfectly habitable, all races speak standard Galactic English. A Vancean hero never bothers to check local physical conditions before disembarking, but he is cognizant of the things that are real in his universe: he checks his handbook for local shibboleths, adjusts his personal symbology to local standards, and registers the local esmeric —the "musty peppery redolence" of the planet of New Concept, for example (*BD*, 18).

Many SF authors get vague and metaphoric when describing the workings of their machines, but Vance is exceptionally so. When Gersen's companion, the mad poet Navarth, muses on the mystery of the Jarnell Intersplit and faster-than-light space travel, the literalist Gersen explains: "Theory dissolves the mystery, though it lays bare a cryptic new spectrum. Quite likely there is an endless set of these layers, mystery below mystery. Space is foam, matter particles are nodes and condensations. The foam fluxes, at varying rates; the average activity of these miniscule fluxes is time." Navarth responds hilariously, "It is all very interesting. Had I followed an early bent, I might have been a great scientist" (*POL*, 117).

Vance's cultures work no better than the Jarnell Intersplit. We know we aren't supposed to ask how they work, but if we defy the implicit directives of the art and ask anyway, we get no answers. The Pnume are a perfect example of this. For at least sixty thousand years Tschai has been inhabited by space-warring races, and during all that time the Pnume have remained symbols of secret terror. In practical terms, they are nothing: silent, cloaked creatures that stand in shadows and live in rabbit warrens. In symbolic terms, they are awesome—because fear of the dark and the underground still remains, unbanished by space travel. On Tschai, where the Dirdir hunters have tracking devices that can find anything, no one can find the Pnume tunnels, because their exits are hidden under boulders and behind trees!

All Vance's peoples share this quality with the races of Tschai, that they live symbolically, not literally. On Trullion, the national sport is hussade, a game between two teams, each represented by a shierl, a female mascot who must be a virgin and who must exude a captivating panache called *sashei*. They are paid nothing. At the end of every match, the shierl of the losing team is ritualistically defiled sexually and abandoned as worthless. Even the least literal-minded reader must wonder, why do the shierls do it? Even Vance asks, but has no answer (*W*, 47, 81). Perhaps it is just the way of Trullion's maidens to be shierls. We can no more account for the act in terms of psychology than we can explain why Envy in the medieval allegory is envious, or why he stands by the road waiting to tempt the questing knight.

Vance frequently offers us models for governmental systems, but these systems are no more than brilliant metaphors or artifacts, facades with no internal workings. *To Live Forever* gives us a world in which everyone seeks "slope," the degree to which one has been awarded an artificially extended lifeline by the few grandees who control the secret of immortality. "Slope" is a wonderful concept, and Vance's interest ends with it as concept; he wisely makes no attempt to work out the logistics of governmental administration. In the Durdane series, the brilliant symbol is the torc, a collar of explosives affixed to the neck of every citizen of Shant at birth to ensure obedience to the Anome; if you stray, the Anome will know and will take your head. But here Vance goes too far: Etzwane sets out to find the Anome and discover how he governs—like David Gerrold peeking behind the *Empire* set to see what the starslug eats. Etzwane finds the Anome, and with him the tools of planetary administration: a button for detonating torcs, a staff of two henchmen, a "packet of vouchers" to handle national finances, and a radio for giving orders to the Discriminators, a group of strongmen somewhere out there (*BMA*, 27-8). Etzwane locks the Anome in his room and takes over. He goes to the office of the head of the Discriminators, announces that the Anome has appointed him to make some changes, and installs a planetary cabinet on the spot. In a marvellously unintentional parody of the transfer of political power, Etzwane fires the head of the Discriminators, appoints himself to the vacant post, and masters his job by pushing a button on the desk, and asking the clerk who responds to explain the function of all the other buttons! (*BFM*, 134). Remember, this is a world in which the particulars of music-making, dining, and docking procedures on the balloon-way are all rendered in meticulous detail.

Vance's cultural psyches, like his governments and his mechanical devices, often turn out to be brilliant, static symbols without guts. Around the planet of Marune four dwarf suns of different colors rotate in complex orbits, producing nine distinct light conditions. Each light condition is represented by a corresponding compelling mood in all Rhunes. Vance charts the nine constellations, names each mood, and discourses on appropriate activities for each period—Chill Isp, for instance, when only blue Dwarf Osmo is above the horizon, "inspires the Rhune with a thrilling ascetic exultation" (*MA*, 43). The time schedule for solar rotations is terribly complex, and the mood alterations are peremptory, so you can imagine the potential for drama here. Vance has fun writing a plot in which the characters' temperaments change with the sudden unpredictability of musical chairs. But he makes almost nothing of this wonderful toy. The Rhunes act like all of Vance's fastidious snobs, without regard to astral conditions, and the conditions effect only one small plot turn and a single encounter (*MA*, 123-4). This inability to bring the symbol to life illustrates why Vance thrives on plot set-ups that stay on the move, letting each brilliant cultural artifact impact the reader, and moving on to new static images. Nowhere does Vance achieve anything like Herbert's Fremen culture or Le Guin's Winter in *The Left Hand of Darkness*, where the single premise infuses and determines every aspect of a fully functioning social or ecological system.

THE IDEA OF A CULTURE

The Fish-God Yob, who seems
as efficacious as any...

Almost all of Vance's fiction addresses a single concept:

culture. What is a culture? Why do sentient creatures make them? How does an established culture change and grow? Are the benefits of living in one worth the drawbacks? Vance's career is a search for answers to such questions.

To the question of *la raison de culture*, the force that shapes it, Vance has three answers: environment, universal needs, and caprice. The last is the one he believes.

Vance often gives lip service to environmental determinism, and argues that social structures are created by environmental forces—Marune, for example, where the culture is supposedly determined by astral physics. At other times, Vance talks of culture as a logical solution to a universal set of problems: staying fed, perpetuating the species, and so on. Ifness, a social historian, naturally sees cultures from this perspective, and praises the disgusting Chilite monks for having devised a solution to the universal questions that is convoluted, effective, and unique. The Chilites are celibate, and so have no offspring; to perpetuate the line, they foster a string of neighborhood prostitution cottages, which provide them with new blood in the form of fatherless boys to serve as acolytes (*An*, 114). Each social group finds its unique means to the same ends.

But the spirit of Vance's writings belies these explanations. For him, culture is primarily a delightful arbitrariness, institutionalized quirkiness, eccentricity elevated to the status of dogma. The Byzantaurs are infuriated by the sight of yellow (*SW*, 53); in the town of Langlin, the sound of "r" is an obscenity (*SF*, 28). Why? Certainly not because the environment or universal need dictates that it be so. For every culture determined by circumstance, in the manner of *Dune*'s ecological imperative, or the equally compelling biological imperative of *The Left Hand of Darkness*, Vance gives us a hundred cultures joyfully undetermined by anything, flying in the face of all logic and all imperatives but one: the need for shared values. Heinlein places his characters on the moon, where the parameters of the environment impinge and demand that they live narrowly within such confines; Vance's action takes place on Big Planet, where the environment merely provides a colorful backdrop to adventures, where population pressure is non-existent and economic needs unnoticed, and where each tribe is free to indulge its individual fantasy and raise a monument to arbitrariness. Thus Vance's definition of culture is the antithesis of determinism; his people worship the note of D flat or the number 5 for no obvious reason, and this lack of reason is essential to Vance's idea of a culture.

In *The Eyes of the Overworld*, Cugel happens upon a village of bestial-looking creatures and fears for his life; but instead he is welcomed as a brother, fed, and outfitted with a boat and supplies. He asks what faith they are. Their leader replies, "We prostrate ourselves before the fish-god Yob, who seems as efficacious as any" (*EO*, 142). Cugel sails to the neighboring village, where he expects a similar welcome from its golden-haired people; instead, he is seized. The leader explains, "We worship the inexorable god known as Dangott. Strangers are automatically heretics, and so are fed to the sacred apes" (*EO*, 144). Cugel is dragged over sharp stones "while the beautiful children of the village dance[d] joyously to either side."

Cugel's experience is the essense of religion in Vance's world, and (since religion is, in a sense, the way a culture accounts for itself) the essense of culture as well. One worships Yob or Dangott, each as efficacious as the other—namely, not efficacious at all, since both are human constructs and projections; and yet both wholly efficacious, as symbols are, at organizing and giving purpose to existence. Gods are powerful because they answer basic questions: Why are we here? Why are we a people, and others are strangers? How should we act? why do we do things this way? What am I afraid of? Why must I die? Ask Yob and the answers flow, and the answers are necessary if men are to cooperate and not despair. Dangott's answers are different, but just as good. People who share a set of answers to the basic questions are a culture; people without answers (Vance's heroes) are condemned to seek them.

Throughout Vance's work, religion is absolutist, absurd, arbitrary, crippling, and destructive. The Funambulous Evangels, the Saltations to Finuka in *Emphyrio*, the ritual gestures of the Theurgic cult in *The Dragon Masters*—"hands palm down to either side, slowly up till the back of the hand touch[es] the ears, and the simultaneous protrusion of the tongue. Over and over again..." (*DM*, 75)—all make the same point: religion contorts the believer into knots and makes him look like a jackass.

Religion hobbles the believer and makes him vulnerable to all pragmatists, as is epitomized by the Battle of Rudyer Moor in *The Face*. Two sects, the Ambrosians and the Aloysians, meet in battle over the resting place of a slab of sacred marble. At sundown, the Ambrosians, according to their creed, break for vespers and "place themselves in devotional attitudes"; the Aloysians, not bound by such strictures, slaughter the spread-eagled Ambrosians, and the war is over (*F*, 16).

And religion exacts a monstrous toll of suffering from the believer, as the Mother of the Gods can attest. The people of Gozed worship the local sea-scorpions. When the scorpions come to land to spawn, a female sacrifice, "the Mother of the Gods," is left on the beach as a host. The scorpions deposit their eggs in the body of the Mother by stinging her. She is then devoured by the hatching larva and dies in religious agony/ecstasy (*SOW*, 41). Adam Reith calls this "an unsettling religion," but Anacho reminds him, "Still it appears to suit the folk of Gozed. They could change any time they choose." They do not change, because the rewards of believing outweigh the terrible cost.

Vance's heroes don't think so. In a round-table discussion about religion, Reith expounds the views of Vance's empiricist outsiders:

> Man and his religion are one and the same thing. The unknown exists. Each man projects on the blankness the

25

shape of his particular world-view. He endows his creation with his personal volitions and attitudes... The correlation between a man and the shape into which he molds the unknown for greater ease of manipulation is exact (*SOW*, 43).

The atheist, Reith concludes, "accepts the cosmic mysteries as things in themselves; he feels no need to hang a more or less human mask upon them." But while Reith and his fellows see the imposing of form on the chaos as an act of weakness, an escape from things as they are, the rest of Vance's people see it as the act that makes civilized races civilized. Anacho the Dirdirman refuses to believe that Earth exists, because the idea violates the pattern he has projected onto the blankness. Reith warns him that one so committed to preconceptions is subject to surprises, which on Tschai are usually fatal, but Anacho replies that such a one "at least has organized the cosmic relationship into categories, which sets him apart from animals and sub-men" (*SOW*, 88). Order, even an arbitrary one, is worth dying for: when the diplomat Hableyat tells the Earther Joe Smith in *Son of the Tree* that he will now kill himself for his diplomatic failure, Joe suggests practical alternatives: Hableyat, who is not practical but is wise, says, "That is not our custom. You may smile but you forget that societies exist through general agreement as to certain symbols, necessities which must be obeyed" (*ST*, 106). When Joaz Banbeck points out to the Demie, the elder of the sacerdotes, that his philosophy is based on factual error, the Demie is not perturbed: "Facts can never be reconciled with faith," he responds, meaning that facts therefore must be ignored (*DM*, 56).

Vance offers us two antithetical ways of living, represented by two archetypal characters, the Man of Culture and the Individual. The Man of Culture *believes*: he gives up freedom and flexibility and accepts a set of beliefs shared by a group of others, beliefs that are usually repressive, absurd, and destructive—he ends by sticking his tongue out over and over like a Theurgic cult automaton. In exchange, he gets stability, community, and answers to all his questions. "All is relative ease and facility in orthodoxy" (*DM*, 59). The Individual refuses to believe without proof, asks embarrassing questions, and seeks personal answers to the big questions; he either becomes a quester, like Gersen, Guyal, and Etzwane—spiritually barren, and striving to fill the void—or a utilitarian animal, like Cugel, who lives to no greater purpose than feeding his appetite of the moment. Vance's questers are robbed of their cultures by others, as Gersen is, or heroically banish themselves from cultures that have grown intolerable, and immediately begin building new ones, as Ghyl Tarvoke does in *Emphyrio*; but Vance is always eloquent on the cost of such freedom of movement. When Dystar argues that he owes obedience to no one, Mialambre refutes him:

"Not so. This is an egotistical fallacy! Every man

alive owes a vast debt to millions—to the folk around him who provide a human ambience, to the dead heroes who gave him his thoughts, his language, his music!.... The past is a precious tapestry; each man is a new thread in the continuing weave; a thread by itself is without meaning or worth" (*BFM*, 156).

Of Vance's two alternatives, the Man of Culture and the Individual, one is based on illusion and the other is sterile. Until Vance's recent novels, which seek a reconciliation between the two, almost all of his plots center around the eternal war between them.

RESPONDING TO A RELATIVISTIC UNIVERSE

Much would depend upon his viewpoint.

In a universe where every region of every planet "considers itself the single oasis of sanity" in a galaxy of heterodoxy and madness (*BP*, 13; *An*, 63; *BD*, 118), how does a sensible person proceed? The Sarkoys consider it a capital crime to throw sour milk on one's grandmother, and are "appalled at the insensitivity" of offworlders who don't agree (*POL*, 63). If this is what Belief is like, what can a wise man believe? Should he embrace a belief system at random, for the sake of answers, or is there an objective truth worth seeking, something transcending local mores? Vance's answers to such questions change as his career progresses. In the early works, like *The Five Gold Bands* and *Slaves of the Klau*, the right thing is to convert alien heathens to Americanism. Earthly heroes go forth to preach progressivism and dynamism to enervated alien peoples mired in dogma or tyranny. "You skinheads can do the square-roots, I'll grant you, but for the good side-man in a rough-and-tumble give me one from green old Mother Earth!" crows Paddy Blackthorn, the hero of *The Five Gold Bands*, sounding nothing like Vance's later heroes (13). This familiar '50s chauvinism may have been mandated by Campbell's editorial policies, but it is resurrected to mar Vance's otherwise superb Tschai series, where Earth scout Adam Reith makes a career of what *Star Trek* calls violating the Prime Directive—he liberates one race of men in each of the first three volumes, exhorting them to throw off their chains, to remember that they are men, and to begin striving for themselves, in an unintentional echo of "The Men Return." The emotional reality of Tschai reveals this balderdash for what it is; Tschai is much richer than anything Reith has to offer it, and we wish that Reith would leave it alone.

More representative of Vance's mature attitude is Ifness, representative of Earth's Historical Institute on Durdane. He and Etzwane journey into the slaving territories of Caraz, where they are attacked by their guides, who intend selling them. The guides are disarmed, and the next paragraph begins in a new locale:

> Etzwane and Ifness continued toward the mud-and-wattle inn, leading the riderless beasts. Ifness said, "Six ounces of silver for two able individuals; it seems no great sum. Perhaps we were gulled..." (*As*, 62).

When in slaving territory, sell slaves. Instead of trying to impose his own view of things on the new environment, as Reith does, Ifness accommodates himself to it, and enjoys the unique esmeric of the place from the inside. In the beginning, Vance feels about culture the way a child feels about food: he chooses a favorite, and wants to expunge all others from the face of the earth. But Vance's mature protagonists are gourmets, seeking to know the full range of eating sensations, and realizing that "liking" is only a sliver in the full circle of experience. There are no "bad" esmerics. From such a perspective, we study alien cultures as scientific specimens, or enjoy them as works of art, but never judge them.

Arthur Jean Cox notes in Vance "the absence of any trace of paranoia," and says that his protagonists *introject* their environments (incorporate them within themselves) instead of *projecting* their worldviews on them and forcing them to conform (*JV*, 80-82). Vance allegorizes this point in an introductory quotation from "The Avatar's Apprentice," in which Marmaduke the acolyte finds himself in a wholly alien environment. Inspection reveals that he is in a gigantic eye. The passage concludes, "The central problem, so it seemed, was to learn from whose eye he looked forth. Much, after all, would depend upon his viewpoint" (*KM*, 152). Marmaduke, like Vance's mature work generally, is comfortable looking through alien eyes. Etzwane, upon arriving at Kahei, the planet of the Ka, immediately begins trying to introject the Ka's symbology, in order to make sense of the alien sensory input (*As*, 141), in contrast to Reith, who maintains his sanity in the Pnumes' tunnels "by sheer brutal energy,..impos[ing] his personal will-to-order upon the...environment" (*P*, 151). Much of Vance's fiction in the Sixties gets its energy from the clash of Marmduke's and Reith's points of view.

The epitome of introjection is Gersen's trip to Sarkovy, where the only art, hobby, sport, and profession on the planet is poisoning (*POL*). The Sarkoy poison because their people have always poisoned; it is simply the thing that they do. We share their pride in their craft, their clinical interest in the state of the art. Gersen's Sarkoy guide Edelrod tells how a venefice became affronted by the coin-tree because it could not be rendered toxic; after great study over several years, he produced "a substance of unusual potency." Edelrod enthuses, "Think of it! From waste, a useful and effective poison! Is this not a tribute to human persistence and ingenuity?" (*POL*, 14) Gersen, a good introjector when not on the hunt, replies, "An impressive accomplishment."

Vance often pairs his non-judgmental protagonists with companions of inflexible value systems who insist on judging one culture by the standards of supposed Rightness. Gersen's companion on Sarkovy is the sheltered princess Alusz Iphigenia of Thamber, who can't believe that the Sarkoys openly devote themselves to "evil." Edelrod explains:

> "We serve a useful purpose; everyone occasionally needs poison. We are capable of this excellence and we feel duty-bound to pursue it...Have you no skills of your own?"
>
> "No."
>
> "At the hotel you may buy a booklet entitled *Primer to the Art of Preparing and Using Poisons*, and I believe it includes a small kit of some basic alkaloids. if you are interested in developing a skill—"
>
> "Thank you, I have no such inclination."
>
> Edelrod made a polite gesture, as if to acknowledge that each must steer his own course through life (*POL*, 15).

The novel shares Edelrod's broad view; when the threesome attends a combination banquet and public execution, demises and dinner courses alternate in the same neutral tone: "The sexual offender tried to kick poison into the undermaster's face and was reprimanded...The sixth course, an elaborate salad, was followed by teas, infusions, and trays of sweetmeats..." (*POL*, 27)

What is intelligence?, asks Marmaduke, and the wise Eminence replies, "A standard which men in their egotism use to measure other and perhaps nobler races, who are thereby dumfounded" (*StK*, 142). A far cry from Paddy Blackthorn.

Beyond even this connoisseur's catholicity lies an emotional truth about culture implicit on every one of Vance's pages. his cultures are steeped in emotional intensity; his heroes are spiritually barren, stripped of esmeric in the pursuit of maximal efficiency. Vance always chooses the esmeric-rich option, and thus must inevitably choose the life of Belief over the life of Individualism.

In Vance, a culture finds its purest expression in a Totem, a huge, ancient, magnificent artifact, the product of countless generations of labor and aesthetic sophistication, the source of monstrous injustice and suffering, the bearer of the culture's sense of wonder and magic, ultimately the physical manifestation of the culture's definition of itself.

A typical Totem is the birth-sac of the Splang in *Slaves of the Klau*. Each Splang wears a sacred charm, called a birth-sac, containing a map of his birthplace, attached to his belly by a leech. The charm gives the Splang his strength; remove it, and he is in your power. Here are the two central paradoxes of the Totem: it combines great beauty and great horror, and it makes the believer simultaneously powerful and impotent.

The Totem consumes most of the culture's energies and is watered with the blood of the citizenry, but the price is worth it, because the Totem gives life glorious purpose. Life's object is to comprehend or increase the Totem, and these tasks are never completed. The sacerdotes' Tand, for instance:

> There was never an end to the study of the tand: new intuitions were continually derived from some heretofore overlooked relationship of angle and curve. The nomenclature was elaborate: each part, juncture, sweep, and twist had its name; each aspect of the relationship between the various parts was likewise categorized (*DM*, 58).

The Tand welds its people together in a bond of community both intimidating and beautiful:

> At his puberty rites the young sacerdote...must construct a duplicate tand, relying on memory alone. Then occurred the most significant event of his lifetime: the viewing of his tand by a synod of elders. In awesome stillness, for hours at a time they would ponder his creation, weigh the infinitesimal variations of proportion, radius, sweep, and angle. So they would infer the initiate's quality,...determine his understanding of Final Sentience, the Rationale, and the Basis (*DM*, 59).

Other Totems include Pharesm's sculpture (*EO*), the Song of the Ka (*As*), the organic houses of Iszm, King Kragen (*BW*), and the torc of Durdane; but the archetypal Totem is the sacred Tree in *Son of the Tree*: twelve miles tall, with a trunk five miles in diameter, the object of worship for the planet Kyril's population of five billion. The Laity serve the Druids, the few priests in charge of the Tree, and in exchange are promised life eternal in the Tree's bosom. The Druids eat on tables polished by the labor of ten men's lives (*ST*, 29), but the Laity get answers to all the hard questions. So it has gone for a thousand years, and the people of Kyril plan to export the system by transplant until every planet can worship a shoot of the Tree and have its questions answered too. The intruder, Earther Joe Smith, discovers the inevitable price tag of orthodoxy: the Tree literally lives off its worshippers, converting the bodies of thousands of eager pilgrims a day into vegetable fiber. The Totem is literally God: that which gives meaning to life and exacts a terrible price.

Into the totemic culture steps the non-believer, who is without horror and without beauty. Men like Gersen or Sklar Hast (*BW*) are without symbols, dress in neutral garb, have no roots, belong to no one, and believe in nothing except "Getting On With It." The atheist destroys the Totem, kills God: Hast kills King Kragen; Joe Smith dumps tons of weed-killer on the Tree; Etzwane removes the torcs and imperils the Song of the Ka. Cugel the pragmatist discovers the creature that Pharesm has labored three hundred years to call forth from Beyond, and eats it!

The atheist liberates the man of culture and impoverishes him, freeing him to join the atheist's quest for meaning by destroying the meaning he already has found. Thus Reith buries Onmale, the emblem-soul of Traz, and Traz joins Reith's journey across Tschai in search of answers. Over and over, Reith acts out this myth of freedom: he kills men's faith, thus freeing them to strive.

Joe Smith makes explicit the jingoistic Americanism of these killers of wonder when he says to a worshipper of the Tree, "On Earth...we'd run a spiral runway around the thing, send excursion trips up and sell hot dogs and soda pop on the top. We'd use the thing, not let it hypnotize us..." (*ST*, 99).

Symbols enslave, freedom impoverishes. One must choose, and Vance chooses belief. The figure of the Earther, who is always the atheist, begins as liberating hero in Vance's career, but soon is revealed to be Satan, the despoiler of dreams. In Vance's late work, his protagonists wage war against the forces of progress and win. Vance's shift in values is revealed in his changing attitude toward slavery: in works like *Klau*, freeing the slaves is an unconditional success story. Similarly, in the Durdane series, when Ifness frees the slaves of the Ka, we focus on Kretzel, an old woman who has served the Ka all of her adult life as keeper of the Great Song; she has now returned friendless and naked to Durdane, where she is without purpose and where no one values the cultural heritage she carries with her. She wanders off to nowhere, and Etzwane weeps for the loss of her servitude (*As*, 190).

CULTURE AS JUNGIAN INDIVIDUATION

He found a dead leaf, put it
in his mouth, and began to chew.

Vance is an artist of the extreme; his worlds, like the sailing ships of Tschai, have "every aspect exaggerated, every quality dramatized" (*SOW*, 37). This is the joy of fantasy generally, where "passions [are] more intense: grief more poignant, joy more exalted" (*D*, 91), where villains are the distillation of evil, and life can be experienced unconditionally, without ambivalence. Vance loves images of obsessive, unconditional, absolute behavior: the Dirdir, who hunt in a trance, controlled by a part of their brains called "Old State," which is irresistible to the Dirdir and their quarry (*D*, 60); the Chasches' noses, which are so sensitive they can smell hunger on a man (*CC*, 101); Golickan Kodek the Conqueror, who rode out of nowhere, made a pile of humanity half a thousand feet high from the populations of two conquered cities, mused on his creation, and rode back (*DE*, 48); the Koton monument called Arma-Geth on the Plain of Thish, where a million slaves polished a fifty-mile square as smooth as a mirror and built titanic statues of Koton heroes in the center —General Khainga plans to expand it until it occupies a fourth of the planet's surface, to house his own statue (*FGB*, 97). The Demon Princes are self-declared artists of extremity: Falusche explores the limits of emotional experience generally (*POL*, 112); Kokkor Hekkus limits himself to the art of terror (*KM*, 67); Larque is a comedian. Vance is in this sense of archetypal Demon Prince, attempting to isolate emotive experience in elemental form: the ultimate sexual encounter, the ultimate nightmare, the ultimate prank, the ultimate meal, the ultimate music....

In pursuit of the maximized and purified sensation, Vance divides complex entities into a number of pure parts. He is a habitual codifier and categorizer, especially of behaviors, moods, and appetites. Even the semi-sentient beasts of Vance's worlds are subject to such analysis: the wild ahulphs of Durdane experience four emotional states, each represented by a particular emitted odor: gregariousness, hostility, and "two varieties of excitement unknown to the human race" (*As*, 77). In Vance's worlds everyone codifies the psyche: Kokkor Hekkus begins his lecture on "The Theory and Practice of Terror" by listing the basic kinds of fear (*KM*, 67). Such codification breaks down experience the way chromatography breaks down enzymes, so we end up with components in perfect, beautifully intense isolation. Each experience in Vance is like eating straight saffron or bathing in the perfume essense of a million violets.

The heart of Vance's model of behavior is that his creatures are in one pure state or another, never a mix of the two—essence of violets or attar of roses, but no blends. In terms of Jungian psychology, Vance is isolating the archetypes, the pure, one-dimensional roles, within the whole multi-dimensional personality. For instance, Transactional Analysis, a popularized application of the Jungian concept, posits three pure archetypes within each of us: the Child, the Parent, and the Adult. Each archetype demands to be expressed and catered to, and our actions and feelings are the disorderly amalgam of the workings of the three. A prime function of fiction, in this view, is to allow the archetypes to indulge themselves unconditionally in a fantasy environment where we don't have to pay the price of such extremism. The process of isolation is called by Jungians "individuation." Vance's fiction puts individuation on an assembly-line basis.

For Vance, one of a culture's primary tasks is to individuate the social psyche, to codify the behavior of its people to label the categories, and to erect a rigid structure of castes, times, and places within which each archetype may be expressed. Sometimes the fragmentation is linked to natural cycles, as in the case of the Khors, each of whom has two souls, one that rises with the dawn and one that takes over at sunset (*D*, 47); or Marune, where the Rhunes' nine moods are dictated by astral conditions. But more commonly the fragmentation is imposed on the population by its culture, as an integral part of the culture's large job of structuring and giving meaning to experience. The nobles of Cath call themselves by a different personal name in each kind of relationship or activity: a flower name (for pageants), a court name, a child name (for one's parents), a friend name, a secret name, and "one other," perhaps never told to anyone (*CC*, 97)—thus Vance's cultures label the selves within the self. Zaccare isolates the functions of life and assigns an appropriate odor to each; Erjelbar labels the basic personality types with musical symbology (*MT*, 104); and other Vancean cultures label the possible emotions with color symbolism. Earth culture also differentiates itself by assigning nurturing to women, play to the young, and lust and aggression to men; Vance carries this process to its logical extreme.

A culture gains power over its members by reining in the energy of the id and making it subservient to the superego, the enforcer of order and discipline. Sex is universally seen as a symbol of id energy, and cultures usually legislate its conduct heavily, telling citizens when, where, and how the energy may be deployed. Vance's cultures do this in absolute terms: typically, sexual energy is banished from daily social activity, and restricted to a ritual time and place where it is obligatory and often performed ostensibly in service to the State's deities. On Marune, lust is unthinkable except during Murktime, the rare periods of total darkness, at which time it is mandatory and peremptory. The Khors deny the fact of sex in their village, but practice unbridled promiscuity during forest sex ceremonies, where ritual masks preserve anonymity and so allow citizens to maintain the myth of pure superego personas at home. Sophisticated cultures usually set up islands of cathartic release, like Carnevalle (*TLF*) and Disjerferact (*W*), where sybaritic chaos rules unchecked within stated boundaries.

Vance's favorite form of psychic fragmentation is the dichotomy, the balanced opposition of antitheses, yin, and yang. The Vancean universe often consists of paired opposites. Sometimes the opposition is manifested in characters such as Adam Reith's travelling companions, Traz (the instinctual one) and Anacho (the hypercultivated one); sometimes in castes, as in *The Blue World*, where workers provide the energy and the priesthood functions as superego/governor of society; occasionally the opposition is within the personality itself, as in the chaotic *awaile* that lurks within each Yao of Cath; but most commonly, the opposition is geographical: the landscape of the world becomes a model of the polarized psyche—each half restricted to its terrain—with distinct borderlines between the two. The dark side is often confined to levels below the surface—for instance, the Pnume, the aquatic merlings of Trullion, or the purple toadthings of Maastricht in *Emphyrio*—creatures that lurk underfoot and suck men under. Lust is commonly banished to pleasure isles, as mentioned earlier. But Vance's favorite model, which dominates the landscape in the majority of his worlds, is the dichotomy between the world of civilization (superego) and the wildlands (id). On one side of the border, social man suffocates under his self-imposed, repressive order; on the other, elemental man steals, kills,

33

makes magic, and copulates in a whirl of passionate intensity.

Implicit in this archetypal model is an assumption that the division is neurotic and that health lies in the integration of the parts; or, if integration is impossible, a healthy exercise of all parts in turn. Vance's dichotomized worlds experience three different ways to resolve the tension between yin and yang: one kills the other, the two co-mingle, or the two rule alternately forever.

If the superego disenfranchises the id completely, sooner or later the id will overwhelm the superego and destroy it in order to win recognition, as in *The Last Castle*, "The Miracle Workers," and all the novels that end with repressed masses rebelling and taking revenge on an exploitative nobility—*Emphyrio*, *The Blue World*, *To Live Forever*. Sometimes sanity is achieved by a melding of extremes: Traz and Anarcho are forced to cohabit and learn from each other; Pao heals its planetary schizophrenia by putting its four languages into the mixmaster and creating Pastiche, a melting pot of the four world-views represented by the languages; in *The Last Castle*, *Emphyrio*, *The Gray Prince*, *Wyst*, the Durdane series, and others, a representative of civilization journeys into the wildlands, is touched by the experience, and returns ready to work toward altering the existing culture through his broadened awareness.

But Vance's typical means to sanity is the alternation of opposites. Two of his finest short stories, "The New Prime" and "The Miracle Workers," are examples of the application of alternative rule.

In "The New Prime," candidates for the position of Prime, or Galactic Ruler, are thrown into a series of imagined alien environments and asked to cope with possible crises there. The candidates' solutions will be scored and a winner chosen. The reigning Prime, who designed the test, demonstrates leadership, courage, resistence to pain, aggressiveness, and imagination, and he assumes he has won. But the judges see more deeply, and explain why he has lost. His virtues, which his test was unconsciously designed to reward, are the virtues of authoritarianism, which may be considered vices from another point of view. The judge explains via an analogy: "If the eagle were conducting a test to determine the king of beasts, he would rate all the candidates on their ability to fly; necessarily he would win. In this fashion the mole would consider ability to dig important..." (205). There is no best beast, no optimal Prime. The current Prime's reign has brought "an irruption of autarchies" to the galaxy, and it is time for a new set of virtues: gentleness, sympathy, compassion. The winner ironically is he who did worst on the test—the mole unable to fly at all—one so sensitive to the brutalities of the test that he has been reduced to blithering. Vance's conclusion drives home the irony: "The new Prime, Lord of two billion suns, found a dead leaf, put it in his mouth, and began to chew." The previous Prime, we are told, was a compassionate man, and we envision compassionate and authoritarian Primes healthily alternating regimes forever.

"The Miracle Workers" makes a similar point. Here a human culture on an alien planet has forgotten the craft of science, and has mastered the art of magic instead. The men are threatened by the First Folk, autochthones who are impervious to magic, which works according to the laws of human psychology and thus doesn't effect alien minds. Faced with extinction, the men "turn their backs on sanity and return to the mysticism of their ancestors" (64)—namely, experimental empiricism. A young, elastic-brained wizard named Sam Salazar stumbles on a chemical means to drive off the First Folk—a truce is declared, Sam and his followers undertake to explore the possibilities of the new/old way of seeing, and the old guard bemoan the new "intellectual anarchy" (84). Sam is a mole judged by eagles, and so deemed feeble-minded, but it's now time to dig, and the eagles must adapt or die.

This concept of alternating absolutes suffuses Vance's work. The Institute may praise Man for being "a thousand gloriously irrational compromises between two thousand sterile absolutes" (*KM*, 38), but for Vance compromise is usually impossible, and one can only juxtapose opposites, oscillating from one to the other. "The Men Return" is based on the metaphor. Ifness acknowledges its truth when he confesses that in order to gain intellectual command of himself he has chosen to lose his instinctual wisdom (*As*, 55). The Connatic acts on the same principle, by purposely refraining from eradicating the starmenters (space pirates) from the Alastor Cluster, on the theory that the civilized worlds' yin needs the starmenters' yang to keep their blood from thinning out (*W*, 221).

The concept achieves symbolic expression in Vance's recent work, *The Book of Dreams*, as charnay, the fruit of bliss and agony. Charnay is the gourmet's ultimate delight, but through its nectarous flesh run veins of mortal poison; the slightest slip in preparation, and the diner dies with much suffering. Not surprisingly, to the reader familiar with Vance, a poison-free charnay could easily be developed, but no one wants one—the proximity of horror adds to the keenness of the ecstasy (*BD*, 65). In other words, yin without yang soon grows stale. The object in life therefore is not to find a sensible compromise between extremes, nor even to pick the extreme one likes best. The main object is to sample all possible extremes, in their ultimate form, without co-mingling them, but in as close a counterpoint as possible.

In these terms, he lives best who lives as many uncompromised lives as possible, and characters in Vance's worlds often do this. Howard Alan Treesong lives richly because he carries seven distinct personalities within him; his dream is to be the Galaxy's King of Thieves and head of the IPCC, the galactic police force, at the same time. But the ultimate success story is that of Kokkor Hekkus, who lives on Thamber, a world of pure, isolated antitheses: "The castles have great halls where the bards sing and pavilions where maidens dance to the music of lutes, but below are dungeons and torture chambers. The knights are a magnificent sight in their armor and their flags, and then in the snows of Skava Steppe their legs are hacked off by the Skodolak nomads, and they lie helpless until the wolves tear them to pieces" (114). Hekkus orchestrates the planet, preserving its primal intensities, and, with the help of his hormagaunt powers, playing all the roles. "An emphatic man lives a hundred lives," he says; "He exults greatly, he suffers greatly, he fears greatly, but never would he arrange matters differently" (77). Gersen says of him, "A single life was insufficient for him; he must drink at every spring, know every experience, live to all extremes" (157). Here is a goal worth striving for! The Demon Prince novels are Vance's only works where he refuses to embrace multiple perspectives or to integrate them into a pastiche of wisdom; here, the hero seeks to kill the passionate side of the psyche and succeeds to his own impoverishment. He spends his life seeking to destroy one half of the yin/yang balance of his own universe, and when he triumphs he feels "deflated." "I have been deserted by my enemies," he elegizes on the last page of *The Book of Dreams*; Kokkor Hekkus and Howard Alan Treesong could perhaps have warned him that one's enemies are merely that part of oneself one hasn't yet learned to enjoy. Instead of drinking at every spring, Gersen devotes his life to capping the springs he has judged to be "bad," and this gives the Demon Prince novels an aura of melancholy self-destruction rare among Vance's works.

Most of Vance's work addresses a single question: how can the needs of the individual—the need to express the self, to grow, to build something—and the needs of society—the need for permanence, stability, security—be reconciled? The individual's needs are dynamic—he wants to *go* somewhere; the society's needs are static—it wants to *preserve*. Vance's work again and again returns to three myths, three kernel plots, in search of an answer: in the first, a stranger confronts an unfamiliar culture and is forced to cope with it; in the second, an ossified, caste-ridden society is revolutionized by an iconoclastic citizen; and in the third, a rich, static culture is preserved from the forces of exploitation by a determined conservationalist.

MYTH #1: THE OUTSIDER

The garments a wealthy vegetable grower might wear to an intimate funeral.

In the myth of the Outsider, a hero—a linear questor—without a culture of his own, pragmatic and relativistic, encounters an alien culture and faces an immediate problem: how can the alien world-view be deduced before it kills him for violation of custom? The hero is often deposited unexpectedly in the new environment, stripped of everything but his wits, and forced to undertake a journey to a distant point of safety—the myth of Odysseus—encountering unfamiliar cultures in rapid series, so that the game of playing by another's unstated rules can be played over and over. Each encounter is a contest between the powers of Belief and Unbelief.

In this myth, the essential cultural act is the making of symbols—the assigning of absolute value to the furniture of the physical world. Red means danger, crossed fingers brings luck, two sticks crossed at right angles are sacred, a necktie on a male is a sign of formality—why? Because our culture agrees that these acts and objects shall carry the import we agree they have. Symbology is arbitrary, so an outsider cannot guess it by logic; and it is absolute, so violating it is usually fatal. The Outsider is weak in one sense—he's blind to the local symbology; but he's strong in another sense—he's able to stand outside the cultural world-view and see it objectively, and so exploit it. It's like playing chess: the Outsider is hobbled by not knowing the rules; the Man of Culture is hobbled by having to obey them. The contest is at the center of *Son of the Tree*, *Big Planet*, *The Houses of Iszm*, *Space Opera*, *Eyes of the Overworld*, the Tschai series, *Showboat World*, the Demon Prince series, and large sections of Vance's other works.

The contest can go one of two ways. Often the outsider wins, because he is one-eyed in the kingdom of the blind. Remember the Battle of Rudyer Moor: if your enemies believe and you don't, you can slaughter them while they are frozen in devotional attitudes. This is the theme of "Coup de Grace," in which trouble-shooter Magnus Ridolph must determine which of seven representatives of different alien cultures murdered Bonfils, the anthropologist. Ridolph considers the value systems of the seven cultures. Fianella of the Thousand Candles, from Journey's End, proffered love to Bonfils and was spurned, and she swore to kill him in defense of her honor; this makes her a strong suspect, but Ridolph has studied the mores of Journey's End and thus knows she's innocent—Bonfils was shot, and Fianella could only win honor by driving him to death with longing for her. All suspects are similarly eliminated, until only the murderer remains: the Bonze, whose people are altruistic philosophers who believe in reincarnation. Bonfils was depressed, so the Bonze killed him as a kindness, to hurry him on to his next, hopefully happier, life. Each culture has its own vocabulary of symbols, and Ridolph is pan-lingual. Reith triumphs in the same way, manipulating the rigid customs of each culture he encounters—the Dirdir particularly—because he can see loopholes the natives (who are too close to their own culture) cannot.

But Vance has more fun when the contest goes the other way, and the Outsider is undone by his unfamiliarity with custom. He spits on the flag—makes an apparently innocent gesture that turns out to break a local taboo. There is no way to deduce the taboos; one village will roast you for spitting on the flag, and the next will roast you if you don't.

Showboat World and *Space Opera* both devote themselves to documenting the inevitability of spitting on the flag. *Showboat World* sends Apollon Zamp's showboat on a tour of the villages along the River Vissel on Big Planet, Zamp's troupe playing before a different arbitrary, treacherous set of local shibboleths at each stop. Before each docking, Zamp consults the River Index, the handbook of regional mores, to find out which flags not to spit on today: at Gotpang Bump the Index reminds him "to make no reference to disease, accident, or death, nor to suggest that birth could be achieved other than through the cooperation of an Actuarian" (17); the Whants interpret yellow as a sexual invitation (42); at Henbane Berm all male roles must be played by women and all female roles by men—"Don't ask me why," Zamp says (88). Zamp is a perfect relativist, determined to speak to each customer in the customer's own language; but he is saddled with a financial backer, Gassoon, who insists that all creatures are one under the skin, and that *Macbeth* is therefore suitable for all audiences. Zamp labors heroically to find a compromise between Gassoon's demands for authentic Shakespeare and the potentially lethal demands of his audiences' symbologies. *Space Opera* pursues the same joke, as Dame Isabel Grayce, a close-minded matron of the arts, tours the galaxy with a troupe of Earth's best performers, trying to enlighten the rubes in the provinces, and refusing to consider the audiences' mind-sets or notice the alien esthetic wonders around her.

Most of Vance's outsiders are simultaneously able to exploit the alien culture and are rendered helpless by it. In "The Moon Moth," Thissell, Earth diplomat to the terrifyingly complex and rule-bound culture of Sirene, is completely immobilized while trying to avoid stepping on cultural toes. He fails until the very end of the story, when he is about to be executed for spitting on one flag too many. He suddenly sees the loophole in the social structure and exploits it, heaping glory on himself with the ease of a burglar who has suddenly found the key to the Mint. On Tschai, Reith can rob, murder, and bamboozle the Dirdir because he knows how they think and can thus manipulate them; but in the super-sophisticated city of Cath he is a blunderer: he tries to dress himself to make a good impression, and is informed that he has, instead, selected "the garments a wealthy vegetable grower might wear to an intimate funeral" (*SOW*, 65). He has an interview with Cizante, the Blue Jade Lord of Cath, where the rules are so subtle that we never find out what they are; Cizante's growing outrage informs us that every sentence Reith speaks fails to conform to some unspecified requirement of decency, and every attempt by Reith to apologize merely breaks more invisible rules (*SOW*, 70 ff.).

A culture customarily surrounds sexual practices with a strict symbology, and Vance's heroes err most egregiously in sexual embraces with foreign females. The finest of these is Cugel's experience in the alternate universe to which Pharesm sends him in his anger. At an inn, he is captivated by a woman. Realizing that the local customs are likely to be highly sensitive in the area, Cugel proceeds with great caution, tiptoeing through a moral mine-field. Is it permissible to do this—and this?, he asks before each act. She assures him repeatedly that local custom is lax and indulgent about sex, and they retire to Cugel's room for a night of "erotic exercises." Cugel is awakened by a visit from a scandalized village elder, who points a...quivering finger through the gloom, and says: "I thought to detect heretical opinion; now the fact is known. Notice: he sleeps with neither head-covering nor devotional salve on his chin. The girl...reports that at no time in their congress did the villain call out for the approval of Yelisea!" (*EO*, 103). Poor Cugel is hauled off to judgment.

MYTH #2: THE ICONOCLAST

*Ignorant of the spiritual benefits
to be derived from self-abasement...*

In the myth of the Iconoclast, a culture suffocated and enslaved by its own societal structure brings forth a questioner. This unique individual seeks answers, and the answers he finds throw his culture into convulsions, causing the old ways to be destroyed in fire and blood, and a new structure begun. The social order is based on a Terrible Secret, through which the priests have been bleeding the believers. The secret is easy to see as soon as one looks for it, and once revealed, makes the old ways seem laughable. In *Emphyrio*, for example, the craftsmen of Amboy have labored for generations to support a race of actual puppets; in *The Gray Prince*, the "Big Joke" of Uther Madduc is that the present lords of the Alouan stole the land from the native Uldras, who stole it from the primitive erjins, who stole it from the animal morphotes—their social order resides on nothing stronger or nobler than the eternal rule of "gimme"; in *The Blue World*, the priests justify their order via the Scriptures, ancient texts which turn out to prove that the population is descended from a prison ship, and that they are all sons and daughters of criminals. The Secret is always a harsh, ugly, egalitarian truth that dispels an ancient, esmeric-rich illusion. Myth #2 describes *To Live Forever*, *The Blue World*, *The Last Castle*, *Emphyrio*, *The Gray Prince*, *The Dragon Masters*, the first two volumes of the Durdane trilogy, "The Miracle Workers," and "Dodkin's Job."

The iconoclast is born with "a void which ache[s] for nourishment" (*DE*, 109), a drive to fulfill himself. Jantiff of Wyst says, "If I don't use [my] capabilities and achieve my utmost then I'm cheating myself," and a listener replies, "If everyone were like you the world would be a very nervous place" (40). Ghyl Tarvoke wants to "stamp his imprint upon the cosmos," and when others point out that they aren't so arrogant, he replies, "You are you and I am I. I am dissatisfied" (*E*, 12). These people are graceless, blunt, plagued by self-doubt, unable to "begin to imagine the direction of [their] existence" (*E*, 137), and "ignorant of the spiritual benefits to be derived from self-abasement," in the fine phrase of *The Blue World*'s chief priest (129). They declare themselves masters of their own fates, disown themselves, banish themselves from their homelands to free themselves of the blinders of their heritage. They ritualistically rename themselves, symbolically declaring their right to forge their own identities. This is not done lightly: the iconoclast is terrified by the enormous consequences of his curiosity, and grieves for the ancient beauty his search destroys. At the very end of *Emphyrio*, when Tarvoke has succeeded in shattering the oppressive social structure he has always loved and hated, he looks over the city now so irrevocably altered, and we are told, "Never had he seen so beautiful a sight" (219). In the end, the iconoclast wins only rootlessness and unease—we last see him standing before an open door, staring wistfully at an unknown future, and declaring that he can't go home again (*LOP*, 90; *MA*, 174). But usually he has rendered everyone in his culture homeless as well, and they all set off towards the unknown together, like Adam and Eve, in a replaying of the myth of the Fortunate Fall.

The iconoclast is usually aided by a population of lepers, disenfranchised folk living either outside the border of civilization or in its depths. In *The Last Castle*, the Lepers hold all the ground but the few castles themselves, and they initiate the revolution. The essence of civilization is structure; the essence of the wildlands, where the Lepers live, is passion, instinct, nature. The conflict between them reenacts the eternal conflict of order and chaos, brains and blood, superego and id, artifice and nature, reason and passion, tragedy and comedy. The latter always wins, and the victory is both a joy—liberation, fresh air, rebirth, restoration of vital potency—and a tragedy— the death of ancient greatness, loss of home, loss of answers larger than personal ones. Sometimes the Lepers storm the walls of civilization and win their franchise by force; sometimes, in a more literal psychological model, the repressed energy within the docile citizenry emerges, "emotion accumulated from childhood, stored and constrained, explode[s]" to ravage the oppressors (*BW*, 72); and sometimes the iconoclast journeys into the wildlands and emerses himself in the instinctual, magical, elemental side of his nature, thus making it a permanent part of his personality before returning to civilization.

THE ICONOCLAST VERSUS ARTIFICIAL SOCIETY

He transmits through me a correct type-8 salute.

Almost every Vance novel has at least one society imprisoned in its own claustrophobic organization: Castle Hagedorn (*LC*), Mornune (*SW*), Cath (*SOW*), Sirene (*MM*), the City of "Dodkin's Job," Methal (*F*). The organization may be a form of adminstrative bureaucracy, as in "Dodkin's Job"; sumptuary laws, as in

Cath; religious ritual, as in *The Blue World*; a hideously subtle and structurally complex language, as in Iszm, Kahei (*As*), and Lekthwa (*SOK*); guilds and castes, as in Amboy (*E*) and Olliphane (*Stk*); or a precise and inflexible symbology of smells (Zaccare—*KM*), music (Eiselbar—*MT*), or color. It's all the same thing: culture as superego, codifying, labeling, and prescribing human behavior so totally that every act is compulsory and ritualized, and individualism is inconceivable.

The attraction of such a culture is obvious: it tells you exactly what to do and how to do it—whatever it fails to prescribe is presumed not to exist. But there are a number of drawbacks. For one, such a system is inefficient: its citizens spend all their energy filling out forms, mastering the language, and maintaining orthodoxy. Alien cultures for Vance are often caricatures of human cultures, and the Dirdir's sexual system epitomizes the inefficiency of too complex a social order. The Dirdir know twelve different styles of male sexual organs, fourteen styles of female organs. Each female style may or may not combine with each male style, depending on the circumstances. Anacho explains the result of this: "As you can imagine, a matter so complicated absorbs a great deal of attention and energy, and, perhaps by keeping the Dirdir fragmented, obsessed and secretive, has prevented them from overrunning the worlds of space" (*D*, 149). The Dirdir have their complexity forced upon them by nature, but men build their own tangles to prevent them from going anywhere.

Culture is inefficient for good reason; in the role of superego, culture's job is to tax the energy of the id—to dam it up, license it, regulate it, tame it, and channel it into service to the State. Vance's world is rich with examples of cultures that legislate against the individual personality, or use conventions to curb passion or sexual energy: the Sirenese, who hide their faces behind conventionalized masks from birth to death; the Tunkers of Mizar Six, who all behave identically and limit themselves to a vocabulary of 812 words, "to protect themselves from the perplexity of wondering about each other's motivations" (*StK*, 83); the Calbyssinians. This is the hoarding of the sperm, the universal notion that id forces are too powerful, too precious, to be let loose.

To keep the id forces curbed, society requires that all activity conform to an impossibly complex and inconvenient set of specifications: Luke Grogatch of "Dodkin's Job," working as a Class D Flunky on a tunnel gang in the bureaucratic nightmare of the City, is required by executive memo to walk four miles every morning to a warehouse to check out his shovel, and four miles back at the end of the day to return it—to minimize loss of tools; the craftsmen of Amboy are forbidden by Guild law to use any patterns, duplicating instruments, or tools other than minimal hand tools in their work; among the Iszic, each caste has its own language to obstruct communication (20), and decorum requires the "transmission of a correct Type 8 salute," or whatever type the precise category of conversation requires, before communication can get underway (59); on Sirene, communication between civilized parties must be in modes of spectacularly baroque periphrasis, and accompanied by virtuosic playing on one of a number of fiendishly difficult musical instruments in one of a number of subtle and meticulously prescribed musical forms, the instrument and the form being dictated by the *strakh* (ineffable prestige) of the speaker and the listener and the nature of the conversation (*MM*). In such cultures, all of one's energy is used up just conversing or working.

But "the most rigid institutions...are the most brittle and most susceptible to attack," as Gavin Waylock, the iconoclast of *To Live Forever*, notes (32). Such cultures are "constrained by punctilio as a rotten egg is held by his shell" (*SOW*, 87), and are just as fragile. They are easily manipulated by anyone free of the constraints, and collapse at the touch of a new idea. Grogatch is the only person in the City who realizes that executive orders must originate somewhere; he sets out to find the source, and discovers that the fountainhead of all new directives in the City is Dodkin, the forgotten custodian overseeing the ticker-tape data machines in the bowels of the civil service monolith. Dodkin has been making small suggestions for improvement, which he includes in the river of data flowing to the higher levels. Grogatch instantly sees the potential in this, gets himself demoted to Dodkin's bottom rank, and inherits the post, putting himself in total command of his government. Gyle Tarvoke need only leave Amboy to discover that the local crafts are worth thousands of times more than the Guilds tell the artisans they are, and the cruel exploitation of Amboy by the Lords becomes obvious. In *The Last Castle*, the connoisseurs of the castles are masters of the mathematics of space flight but refuse to touch a tool, and the barbaric meks overwhelm their splendidly refined structures by burying them in mountains of dirt.

The operative word in describing all these cultures is "subtle," a word Vance uses in every novel he has written, usually many times. Denied emotional intensity, these people turn inward and pursue refinement, perfecting niceties as an ice skater polishes her compulsory figures, splitting hairs like Talmudic scholars. On Marune, the nobility practice their "cogences," minute areas of expertise, and compile "dissertations, contradictions, and reconsiderations of these same dissertations; and reconsiderations of the contradictions and contradictions of the reconsiderations—all indexed and cross-indexed" (89). The nobles of Castle Hagedorn are "connoisseurs of essences" (i.e., odors), and have bred Phanes (gossamer, fragile sylphs) as objects of display for thousands of years (*LC*, 63). The dancing that Adam Reith witnesses at Sivishe epitomizes the style:

> The music...seemed to Reith peculiarly simple and limited...A few folk danced: men and women, face to face, hands at sides, hopping carefully from one leg to the other. Dull!...Yet, at the end of the tune the couples separated with expressions of triumph...As minutes

passed, Reith began to sense complexities, almost imperceptible variations...Perhaps, thought Reith, these almost-unheard quavers and hesitations were the elements of virtuosity... (*D*, 106).

Such a system is inherently unjust—the Iszic devotion to tree-house culture keeps a billion earthers living in hovels (109)—but, worse, it's unhealthy. Vance's societies of "connoisseurs, collectors, and aesthetes" (*E*, 191) have lost contact with the soil, the sea, the blood. The Lords of Amboy come down from their sterile eyries to attend local festivals, be seduced, and generally experience human feelings vicariously; Shanne, Tarvoke's noble lover, says to him, "I do so love the ground! Here are the strong things, the passions! Oh, you are so lucky!" (*E*, 129). The effete culture, in an attempt to lock out the chaotic energy of the id, have merely locked themselves in, in what Jacob Nile the doubter calls "the Citadel Complex" (*TLF*, 117). In *The Book of Dreams*, the Institute, quoting a philosophical discussion in *The Gray Prince* (51ff.), expounds on the theme: "Urbanized men and women experience not life but the abstraction of life, on ever higher levels of refinement and dislocation from reality."

"Consider a creature whose every sense, capability, and instinct have been shaped by the natural environment, by interaction with sun, wind, clouds, rain; the look of mountains and far horizons; the taste of natural food; contact with the soil. What happens when this creature is transferred to a synthetic environment? He becomes intellectualized and incompetent. Confronted with a real challenge, he...curls into a ball..." (74-5).

In Vance's world, the antidote is always just across the border.

THE ICONOCLAST IN THE WILD WORLD

The acrid odor of dragon-sweat.

It's called Beyond in the Demon Prince novels, Caraz on Durdane, Balad on Wyst, Maastricht in *Emphyrio*, the Palga plateau in *The Gray Prince*, nomadland in *The Last Castle*—the outback, the antithesis of civilization. It's a world of immediate, passionate intensity: in Cath, to kill someone you hire the Guild of Assassins to adminster the Ritual of the Twelve Touches, a matter of many days and much protocol; when Issam the Thang, one of Vance's frontier types, wants to kill, it's "a knife in the dark, a single sound, and who is the wiser save Issam the Thang?" (*D*, 79).

It's a world of comedy. No one laughs in Vance's sophisticated cultures, since laughter is the human response to life's refusal to make sense, and places like Cath have brought all aspects of life under meticulous control. Thus the triumph of the Outback over the world of Artifice often takes the form of a

Big Joke: Amboy's craftsmen slaving to enrich puppets, *The Gray Prince*'s "Big Joke" that the rulers of the Alouan rule by might alone, or the people of the Floats worshipping the rectitude of their forefathers, who were all crooks.

It's a world of magic and other sources of non-rational wisdom, where witches, ghosts, talismans, and medicine men still have efficacy and are listened to with respect.

Above all, it's the domain of the *picaro*, the rogue thief. Thieves, Vance's symbol of the id triumphant, are clever, quick, appetitive, amoral, independent, and joyously, unabashedly self-indulgent—the antithesis of primness, rectitude, orthodoxy, subtlety, sanctimoniousness, and reserve. Raffles the Cracksman recites the Thieves' Creed: "Money lost, little lost; honor lost, much lost; pluck lost, all lost" (*KM*, 84). Hence the opposition between the thief and the Man of Culture, like Dordolio of Cath, to whom honor (propriety) is everything and pluck is an extinct concept.

Unlike the sophisticated cultures, where outsiders strain to sensitize themselves to refinements on the very threshold of perception, wilderness cultures are a sensual assault. Food curls the tongue; the "acrid odor of dragon-sweat" (*DM*, 22) fills the nostrils, along with the smell of "poorly cured leather, resin, musk" (*P*, 69). These are worlds with "a rough ripe redolence" (*DM*, 39). Artifacts are made by hand and operated manually, and the dung merchant is a respected calling (*SOW*, 26). There is an intimacy with the sea and other elemental stuff: Jantiff of Wyst escapes from the city and flees to the seacoast, where he gathers shellfish in the rough surf and cohabits with a silent witch girl in an abandoned shack.

This world always wins in its war with the world of Artifice; the reality of passion destroys the myth of reason and order. The men of Culture are forced to acknowledge their dark side, and in so doing banish ease and recover feeling. When Sklar Hast succeeds in destroying the repressive tranquility of thirteen generations of float dwellers, his lover says, "It seems that over all these years we have been living dreams. The Floats were so easy and fertile that no one has ever been forced to work or think or suffer" (*BW*, 130). In Vance's value system, the recovery of emotional intensity is worth any price; there is no greater horror than the inability to feel, which is why the Puppet Lords of *Emphyrio*, who literally can't feel, have a pathos about them that is uniquely poignant among Vance's villains.

MYTH #3: HOME

Slabs of resin-impregnated lichen.

Vance's third myth appears only in his recent work, but it dominates it. The new direction is both revolutionary and a logical result of his career-long energies. Until 1973, almost every Vance novel found it necessary to overthrow its central culture or watch it atrophy; but in *The Gray Prince*, Vance reveals a new order: the novel follows Myth #2, but the social order of Koryphon doesn't fall; almost every novel published since then—*Trullion*, *Marune*, and *Maske* especially—centers around a culture that is well and plans to stay that way.

In the myth of home, a member in good standing of a tranquil, organic, healthy culture is threatened with the loss of his heritage—villains rob him of his memory (*MA*), steal his ancestral home (*T*, *MT*), or attempt to "develop," in the realtor's sense, a treasured piece of the family estate (*MA*; *T*). The protagonist recovers his heritage and drives off the entrepreneurs. Gone is the yin/yang balance between the status quo and the forces of change, between Culture and the Individual, between stability and flexibility: Vance has made his choice. The status quo is now healthily static, and the strivers are despoilers (Ramus Ymph of Maske), cads (Rianlle of Marune), or fools (the Fanschers of Trullion). They are defeated rather effortlessly by the forces of tradition, and in the end seem to have posed no real threat at all: the Fwai-chi, an ancient race of wise autochthones, administers a native potion that restores Efraim's memory and reveals Rianlle's perfidy (*MA*); the Fanschers settle on land sacred to a gypsy tribe and are slaughtered as trespassers (*T*); Ramus Ymph threatens the sacred groves of the Wael, a group of tree-worshippers, and they turn him into a tree (*MT*).

The late novels are low in energy; Vance seems tired. His protagonists have no itch needing scratching; they sit on their porches and move only when their right to sit there is threatened. The esmeric of these works rings deeply but tranquilly; the canvas is uncrowded, with little to dazzle the eye.

Although only the last few of Vance's novels follow Myth #3 closely, in restrospect, the emotional truth it expresses is everywhere apparent in his early work: that in Vance's world, value always ultimately lies in organicism and in the past.

Vance's psychically nourishing cultures are always organic. People travel by beast-drawn wagons, by sail or balloon; they trade in "drugs and tinctures, bales of lacy cloth, dried fruit in cakes" (*CC*, 90); they eat "dried fish, sacks of tubers, rolls of pepper-bark, fresh and preserved fruit" (*SOW*, 112); when they fight, they fight with their hands, with poisoned fingernails, with "kick-knives," even when power pistols and other soulless high-technology weapons are at hand; artifacts are made from resin, chitin, and membranes. These worlds are alien, but they are the antithesis of SF's conventional "city of the future" stuff: they are made of alien soil, alien seas, alien fungi, and alien strong physical sensation.

A few of Vance's works take place in primitive environments where he has little choice but to build with resin and eat dried fish. Big Planet has almost no metal, so Zamp's showboat has its drive axle re*glazed* and its *glands* repacked (*SW*, 14). *The Dragon Masters* takes place on a primitive landscape of rock and vetch, where walls are panelled in "lignified reed" (5), torches are made from luminescent algae (51), houses are built of "slabs of resin-impregnated lichen" (35), and so on. *The Blue World* is Vance's virtuoso demonstration that he can make *anything* "using only ash, wood, water, and sea-stuff" (140): Sklar Hast's people make iron and electricity from these things. But in these novels, Vance has no choice; his preference for organic materials and lifestyles shows most clearly in those worlds where any degree of technological sophistication is available to his characters, and they choose to avoid it or hide it. On Tschai, most of the races have been travelling from star to star for thousands of years, yet aircars have balustrades, joy sticks, and engines that knock. Reith goes to a fine hostelry, bathes, and is massaged dry with "handfuls of fragrant moss" (*SOW*, 121). The Basics, who command weapons that can vaporize rock mountains, arm their warriors with antique pistols and swords (*DM*, 76). Beauty Dasce, master of sadism in *The Star King*, favors "a red-hot iron in your ear" (148), in a future culture of a thousand space-going races, where irons logically shouldn't even exist any more.

Vance's characters know that all the magic, all the spirit, lies in things elemental and primitive. Edelrod the Sarkoy explains that all Sarkoy poisons are derived from organic materials, because they work better; Gersen suggests this is merely a matter of chemical purity, but Edelrod holds up "a minatory finger": "Never scoff at the role of the mind!" (*POL*, 14). Kokkor Hekkus allows the knights of Thamber only swords, because there is no emotional intensity in an energy beam (*KM*, 115). Apparently, Vance has lived his life by the same principles, having pursued the careers of potter, musician, sailor, and carpenter.

The logical culmination of such a value system is biomechanical technology, where machines are grown, and Vance has a good bit of it (*StK*, 53; *An*, 65; *LC*, 38). The triumph of such thinking is *The Houses of Iszm*, Vance's boldest statement of the spiritual richness of organic living. The Iszic for 200,000 years have bred, nurtured, and worshipped their line of treehouses. The living houses are sensitive to the thoughts of their owners. They have sphincters for doors, sprout pods that conform to the body when one wants to sit, and provide showers from membranes of aromatic liquid. At its worst, biomechanism sounds a bit too much like Fred Flintstone, but Vance's heart is in it, and it comes alive for us. Aile Farr, typical earther literalist/pragmatist, is blind to the spiritual beauty of the trees, and wants to mass-produce the seeds to solve Earth's housing problem; Zhde Patasz, tree-grower, tries to explain, and despairs: "I cannot speak. Your language has no words to tell what an Iszic feels for his house. He grows it, grows into it. His ashes are given it when he dies. He drinks its ichor; it breathes his breath..." (38). Mass production won't work, because it ignores the essential ingredient of *worship*: "We sing incantations to sprouting seeds," says Patasz; "The seeds sprout and prosper. Without incantations they fail. Why? Who knows? No one on Iszm" (36). But Vance knows why: because the incantations acknowledge the esmeric, without which seed—and life—are barren. Not surprising that in *Maske* Vance rehabilitates his villain by turning him into a tree.

THE PULL OF THE PAST

*The recollection of a million
tragedies, a million triumphs.*

Vance's other unshakable source of value is the past: home, which is the seat of one's personal past; and culture, which is the seat of one's racial past. Vance's works are anchored in symbols of ancient tradition and unbroken lineage: the Song of the Ka (*As*); Morningswake, the ancestral home of the Madducs in *The Gray Prince* and the result of eclectic additions by two hundred years of Madducs; the Djan rugs, which are classified by the number of lifetimes of labor that went into their making (*MT 5*); and, richest symbol of all, Mother Earth, Home of homes, ultimate root of all lineages. Vance's first novel, *The Dying Earth*, is suffused with grief at Earth's passing; *Introduction to Old Earth* discourses on Erdenfreude, the unique and inexplicable euphoria that Earth's stupefying esmeric has on human outworlders visiting Earth for the first time (*POL*, 44); when Ghyl Tarvoke visits Earth, he locates the source of the emotion:

> Each trifling area of soil exhaled a plasm: the recollection of a million tragedies, a million triumphs; of births and deaths; kisses exchanged; blood spilled; the char of fire and energy; songs, glees, incantations, war chants, frenzies. The soil reeked of events; history lay in strata, in crusts...At night, ghosts were common, so Ghyl was told (*E*, 192).

Even in the novels that feel the pull of the heroic quest most strongly, Vance's heroes and villains attest to the primacy of the past over the future. Reith deals with each major race on Tschai, but saves the Pnume, the oldest, the original inhabitants, with a seven-million-year-old recorded past, as his final test. Etzwane in rational terms seeks fair and strong governments for Shant, but in emotional terms, he's searching for his missing father. Keith Gersen's quest is only undertaken because the Demon Princes destroyed his roots by kidnapping his entire village; Gersen spends the entire series mourning the loss, striving to punish the killers of his past, and trying to find a new home. In each of the first three novels, he finds a version of the Garden of Eden, Man's original unspoiled home, and violates it in order to destroy a Demon Prince; in *The Face*, he finds a home he wants, dreams of his children drawing strength from the homestead, is denied entrance, and joins with the villain to punish those who frustrate his dream (176); *The Book of*

Dreams is an unsatisfactory close to the series largely because his search for new roots is awarded no closure there.

Vance's villains agree with his heroes about what matters most. The Demon Princes boast of lavish schemes of self-aggrandisement and plunder, but in fact their primary business seems to be to repair their pasts or build new ones to replace the inadequate lives they had. Malagate the Woe, terror of the known universe, is trapped by Gersen because he lusts after a planet Gersen owns, a world which nearly duplicates Malagate's home; Malagate is a renegade, excommunicated from his people, and is thus destroyed by his desire to return home with his sin wiped clean. Viole Falusche devotes his life to reproducing his first love, Jheral Tinzy, a high-school flirt who jilted him; he has remained celibate throughout his life, waiting for the moment when the latest Jheral will love him. Lens Larque tries to buy a home, is refused, and is revealed to Gersen by his plot to take vengeance on those who denied him. Treesong, the last of them, is the most explicit: *The Book of Dreams* presents itself as a novel about Treesong's plot to become Emperor of the Galaxy, but this business turns out to be trivial compared to what *really* matters to him: he plots to return home for his high school class reunion and rectify all the injustices inflicted upon his pathetic pubertal self by his contemptuous peers. Leopold Friss told the young Treesong to "kiss his arse"; Treesong forces Friss to kiss the "arses" of six pigs in front of the reunion assembly (163). One might think a super-villain would have more important things to do, but Vance's people don't—they gravitate to childhood neuroses and inadequacies with the inevitability of Freudian psychoanalysts.

Throughout Vance's fiction, "home" is the root of the soul. The Myth of Home merely gives in utterly to its pull. In the beginning of Vance's career, the earther is obligated to bring the light of progress to the heathen outback; and, in the process, tramples fragile alien cultural beauty beneath his feet without hesitation. In the middle of Vance's career, the paradox of the Fortunate Fall dominates: the joy of questing and the beauty of the past both tug at us. The past is inevitably sacrificed in the name of progress—but, just as inevitably, we mourn its passing. In his most recent works, Vance releases his characters from any such obligation to welcome progress, and gives them instead permission to stay home and guard the fort from all meddlesome heroes with misguided intentions.

III
VANCE'S WORDS

*Supple sentences, with first and second
meanings and overtones beyond.*

Vance is for word-lovers. He is one of the very few SF writers for whom the How of his medium is more important than the What of his message; a reader who reads for the What—plot, character, idea—as most literature trains us to do, discovers too late that what he has been reading *through* is for Vance the stuff of the fiction itself; and that things like plot, character, and ideas are often little more than frames to support the word-play.

Vance's style is baroque, convoluted, intentionally ponderous, and obfuscatory. In this world, one does not agree; one "gives the most emphatic of corroborations" (*StK*, 82) or "makes complaisant acquiescence" (*StK*, 96). One does not say things; one "utters asseverations" (*BW*, 80). When asked to stop awhile, one says, "I would not be averse to such a sojourn, but in all candor, I travel in penury, and would be forced to seek some sort of gainful employment" (*EO*, 72). One says "What is his semblance?" when he means "What does he look like?" (*EO*, 77). And when one asks a youth to do something, he replies, "You'd have to supplicate my father" (*T*, 132). This is the sound of Vance making simple thoughts complex.

If we approach him from conventional standards and expectations of "good prose," he's a horrid writer: wordy, redundant, often grammatically incorrect, awkward, and impenetrable. But Vance isn't seeking to be clear or correct. This isn't the SF of Campbell, Heinlein, and Asimov, where the value is all in the idea, and the aim of the prose is to explain until maximal communication is attained. Vance's effects often depend on our *not* comprehending, and if we understand too well, the magic disappears. Vance is in the business of making emotive soups, and he thickens the broth with words. If we strip the stock, it will be pale, thin, and tasteless. There is often little behind Vance's words, but the verbal surface itself is of infinite interest. For most SF writers of the '50s, language is merely a way of getting it said; for a few others, like Sturgeon or Bradbury, it is a way of creating an emotional intensity; but for Vance, language is the stuff of life—a fascinating game, an absurd joke, a treacherous delusion. It is the ultimate subject matter of his art—not life as reflected in language, but the life of language itself.

Vance often warns us not to be in too much of a hurry to

read past the language medium. Lorcas of Marune speaks for the Vancean priorities: "Here was the milieu he loved: conversation! Supple sentences, with first and second meanings and overtones beyond, outrageous challenges with cleverly planned slip-points, rebuttals of elegant brevity; deceptions and guiles, patient explanations of the obvious, fleeting allusions to the unthinkable" (112). And in "The Avatar's Apprentice," the apprentice observes that the Eminence's wisdom makes no sense, and the mage replies, "The way along the Parapet is not to the forward-footed" (*StK*, 142). If we keep Lorcas and the Eminence in mind, we will read Vance in the spirit in which he has written.

Vance chooses to write in this manner. He has full command of the alternate style of lean, axiomatic terseness: "He never repays a favor and never forgets a wrong" (*KM*, 19); "Dirdir motives are seldom subtle. They want to ask a few questions and then kill you" (*D*, 117). Vance often uses the terse style in counterpoint to the ornate, to make a point that only works if he is in complete control: here's Smade of Smade's Planet explaining to an interviewer how he maintains order at Smade's Tavern:

> "I say, Gentlemen, please desist. Your differences are your own; they are fugitive. The harmonious atmosphere of the tavern is mine and I intend it to be permanent."
> "So then they desist?"
> "Usually."
> "And if not?"
> "I pitch them into the sea" (*StK*, 5-6).

And finally, all ornament disappears in scenes of battles and other hectic activity (*SOK*, 107-8 e.g.), and in Vance's moderately "hard-boiled" detective fiction.

LANGUAGE AS REALITY MAP

Any organization of ideas presupposes
a judgment on the world.

Vance is fascinated with language as shaper of the universe it describes, the tool that controls the user. Language, in this sense, is a map of reality, an abstracting model that interprets symbolically and imposes organization on the thing it maps. Thus it is like a mirror that creates the image we think it merely reflects. A language teaches its speaker to see experience in terms of the structure the language imposes on it. Modern semantics and entire programs of psychological therapy are based on this notion, that language programs our way of seeing the world and ultimately creates the world we experience. The concept permeates Vance's fiction, and is the focus of *The Languages of Pao*. There, the population of the planet Pao is mired in a lethargy that is part of the national character. Pao is threatened with military attack from a neighboring planet, and in a desperate attempt to instill fighting spirit in its people, Pao's ruler hires the scientists of the Breakness Institute to do something.

The scientists conclude that Pao is inert because its language is inert—you are whatever your language implicitly teaches you to be. They divide the population into three groups, and teach each group a new language contructed to instill a particular world-view: one for the military, one for industry, and one for the commercials. The language of commerce is "a symmetrical language with emphatic number-parsing, elaborate honorifics to teach hypocrisy, a vocabulary rich in homophones to facilitate ambiguity," for instance (57). An Institute instructor explains the rationale behind the experiment:

> "No language is neutral...Every language imposes a certain world-view upon the mind. What is the 'true' world picture?...First, there is no reason to believe that a 'true' world-picture, if it existed, would be a valuable or advantageous tool. Second,...'truth' is contained in the preconceptions of him who seeks to define it. Any organization of ideas whatever presupposes a judgment on the world" (81).

But the experiment works too well, the three populations become fanatical, obsessive, and paranoid, and sanity is restored when the protagonist reunites the people with a new national language, a pastiche of linguistic traits from the other three.

If the Institute can build a language to make its speaker see the world any way it wants him to, what world-view is fostered by Vance's language? What way of seeing is the Institute scientist named Vance instilling in an unsuspecting, malleable readership? As we observe a number of means by which Vance creates his unique verbal aura, we will pause occasionally to ask, "what is the effect of these stylistic features on our individual perceptions of Vance's personal world-map?"

CREATING THE ALIEN AURA

Having to do with slag.

How does Vance create alien worlds with English words? Most obviously, he uses rare words, words known only to master vocabularists: larmoyance, lenticular, lacrymose, eczematous, dystrophic, vulpine, otiose, factitious, stertorous, sebaceous, rugose, vermifuge, vesicant, neurasthenic, carpulous, saprophyte, cyanotic, occult (as a verb), involute, etc. Such words are often from technical or scientific jargons: "rugose" is a botanical term meaning "wrinkled"; "cyanotic" is medical terminology, meaning "dark blue"; "to occult" is a scientific synonym for "to hide"; "involute" is a botanical term for "complex." But in Vance these words aren't doing what we expect them to do. In SF especially, such technical jargon is used to establish a "scientific" tone; they are proof that the users really know their science. Thus, in *The Moon Is a Harsh Mistress*, Wyoming Knott says her figure looks *nulliparous*, meaning she looks like she's never had children (Berkley, 1966; p. 33); and Wells' Time Traveller says, "I won't say a word until I get some peptone into my arteries" (*SF Hall of Fame IIA*, p. 392), in both cases to establish their credentials. They've done their homework, and can hold their science with anyone.

Vance doesn't seek the "nulliparous" effect. For one thing, almost everyone in Vance's worlds uses such a tone, and they aren't scientists at all: gypsies of the wild steppes say "Allow me at least a contravention" (*T*, 130); filthy innkeepers say they will stable horses "provided that you can make suitable recompense" (*As*, 64); a slave-camp remnant explains why one should do the owners' bidding by saying, "Your inducement is persistence of life" (*As*, 145).

In addition, in Vance, we needn't know what the words mean to respond correctly to them. We can only appreciate Wyoming Knott's word choice if we recognize the word as the medical way of saying "having had no children," but we respond best to Vance's words when we don't know what they mean or what social level or profession they represent. They often define themselves by context, or are paired with a synonym. "Is there...no ancient tablet or set of glyphs?" says one (*EO*, 39), and "tablet" helps us gloss "glyphs" without having to reach for a dictionary. When Vance tells us that a *library* contains a "voluminous pandect" on magic spells (*EO*, 51), we may safely assume that a *pandect* is some kind of compendium. When Vance mentions *cloisters* in which live "a *fraternity* of cenobites" (*StK*, 17), we know all there is to know about "cenobite"—it means "member of a communal religious order."

When context doesn't help and we do have to reach for our dictionaries, the dictionary's information often proves irrelevant. Often Vance's hard words add no meaning to the text. He refers to "scoriaceous slag" (*As*, 141), but *scoriaceous* means "having to do with slag"—slag-like slag, in other words. And Vance may use his words *despite* their meanings, not because of them. He uses "dystrophic" to mean evil or twisted, though the dictionary says it means "undernourished" (*KM*, 42); he uses "scarify," a medical term meaning "scratched," to mean "razed" (*TLF*, 6); and "impudicity" (boldness) to mean "lust" (*SOT*, 91). Vance thus will use the wrong rare word to avoid using the right common one: when one studies a manuscript, Vance speaks of his "lucubrations" (night-time study by lamp-light), despite the fact that the examination is by daylight, because he wants to avoid the common word "examination" (*SOW*, 93).

Vance always avoids the commonplace. Here is a partial list of his idiosyncratic terms, and their more familiar synonyms in parentheses: accredit (believe), canon (custom), ilk (tribe), succor (help), minatory (menacing), squamous (scaley), phthistic (consumptive), lucent (luminescent), manciple (servant), sept (tribe), cachetic (emaciated), utile (useful), icterine (jaundiced), wain (wagon), plait (weave), hetman (captain), sigil (seal). He always replaces the emotively neutral word for a synonym pregnant with what he likes to call "immanence." Thus boats are never boats; instead they're cogs, coracles, lighters, barks, or ketches. Alphabets tend to be "syllabaries," not because Vance wants to make the fine distinction between one and the other, any more than he wants to distinguish cogs from lighters, but because the latter evokes the exotic.

Similarly, Vance uses archaic diction a great deal—"batten" for "feed," "countenance" for "tolerate," "raven" for "devour," "pursuivants" for "followers," "bottom" for "ship"—but if we recognize such words as Shakespearean, they don't quite work, for reasons we'll discuss shortly.

Vance knows a number of ways to instill a sense of immanence in words we know pretty well. He often uses words in their etymological or root meanings. He uses "unctuous," which we know to mean offensively flattering, in its original sense of "oily" when he speaks of "unctuous ripples" of water (P, 53); "panache" is used literally to mean "ornamental plume" (LC, 68); "candid" to mean "pure" (StK, 142); "rote" (which means "memorization" to most) to mean "law" (BP, 92); "diaper" to mean "linen fabric" (EO, 164). In each case, we are forced to understand *against* our familiarity with the word, to meet the word freshly, and this is at the heart of the way we know words in Vance's style. Similarly, Vance likes to use words in slight violation of correct grammar, misusing them to make them born again. "I innovate a welcome reform," one says (DE, 141), changing "innovate" from an intransitive to a transitive verb by giving it an object. He uses abstractions to mean concretions: he uses "latency," which means "hiddenness," to mean "hidden *things*" (POL, 126); and "startlement," which should mean "the condition of being startled," to mean "something that startles one" (W, 215).

He likes to force a word to function as an alien part of speech: "I am aware of *bodes*" (GP, 87); "a viscous *seethe*" (NP, 194), and "*blurts* of flame" (W, 209) are verbs used as nouns. He mistreats uncountable nouns, pluralizing them or prefacing them with an illegal article: eruditions, expertises, a competence, despairs, and disgusts. He adds unfamiliar suffixes to familiar roots: bogglement, dubeity, lethality.

But the words that most contribute to Vance's unique aura aren't in any dictionary: expansible, monstance, varmous, stimule, pleasances, sorcelment, and so on. These are Vance's own coinings, built from usually recognizable English parts, sometimes by an approximation of English morphological rule, often by Vance's own compelling mad logic. These words are customized: not built from scratch, but rather stock parts assembled to express a personal eccentricity. Here are some of his finest, followed by a best guess at their intended meanings in parentheses: steading (homestead), conspectus (survey), distrait (distraught), indigenes (natives), conduce (lead), poinct (puncture), autarchy (autocracy), irredemptible (unredeemable), carcery (jail), inducent (inducement), siccant (dry), alimentation (eating), acerb (acerbic), effectuant (nostrum), lume (light), percept (perception). The list is endless, but the technique is clear: Vance chops off suffixes or adds them on, mixes the root of one word with the suffix of another, and so on. Sometimes he makes portmanteau words by combining two words: he calls the steps of a magic spell "pervulsions," from "permutation" and "convulsion."

This process produces some of Vance's best proper names: the Palliatory (hospital), Godogma (a god), the Retent (land held against the barbarians), the Ecclesiarchs (ruling priests), the Tutelars (police), the Whelm (space police).

Many of Vance's words are made from whole cloth, pure coinages. Such words aren't hard to make or even unique to Vance, and his art is only special for the abundance of them. His flora, for instance: thyse, ebane, chanterbells, sparnum, rockwart, zogma, cassander, junkberry, jossamer tree, green-gum, dragon-eye, gadroon, vandalia, gonaive, langtang, barchnut, *ad infinitum.*

To make up words is not difficult; to make up words that carry just the right scent, that strike the reader as new and familiar simultaneously, is extremely challenging, and Vance is a master at it. In a list of performing artists in *To Live Forever*, Vance mentions "aquafacts" and "chronotopes" (30). We're never told what they do, but their roots suggest they are manipulators of water and time respectively. Our imaginations must supply the liquid castles and temporal vortices such artists might produce. Vance's best creations leave English poorer for the lack of them: his term for magical volume is "libram," a word built on the Latin *libra* (book), as in *library*, with an *-m* suffix that brings associations of learning, age, and authority by its similarity to in words like *sanctum*, *compendium*, *theorum*, and *vellum* (parchment). A libram, then, has the connotation of being an old, authoritative collection of wisdom on parchment.

Vance is more concerned with how words *sound*, and the connotations of those sounds than with what they *really* mean. The Rhunes of Marune practice "cogences," trivial areas of expertise. The association is with "cogent," but "cogent" doesn't mean knowledgeable; it means forceful. No matter; the word *means* wrong but *sounds* right—a good epitaph for Vance's use of language generally.

THE REALITY MAP: PART I

A large statement, possibly
of no startling novelty.

What do these features suggest about the shape of the world

Vance wants us to perceive? For one thing, it is a world familiar and alien at the same time—a world in which familiar things are named with alien words, words which have been nudged from their familiar forms to transmit a sense of the eldritch.

Vance, like all creators of alien landscapes, faces a problem: the alien world must strike the reader as new and familiar, alien and comprehensible, simultaneously. It's the problem of Dystar's legendary music again: if the world seems too alien, the reader can't respond to it, and the fiction ceases to have organized impact; Herbert's *Whipping Star* is a good example of this happening (on purpose, in Herbert's case). Yet the world cannot be too recognizable or it will seem mundane. Vance solves the paradox of instantly recognizable alienity with his use of language. His vocabulary is both English and alien, English words used in unEnglish ways, English words no English speaker uses, or alien words built of recognizable English parts. Vance's problem is something like the problem faced by creators of extrapolated futures, who must find a form of English which is both recognizable, communicative, and obviously an extension of present-day English—what English might become if known patterns of linguistic change continue. But Vance doesn't want his English to be the linear product of familiar processes of change working on the English we know, because the connection between his fictional world and our real world is not simply one of extrapolation—his world is *another* world, and so cannot be visibly derivative from modern English in any systematic way. It must instead be English as alien minds would use it to describe unearthly things.

This accounts for Vance's methodical avoidance of the expected word—why he speaks of a lens that "bloats and augments" what one looks at, instead of the obvious "magnify" (*EO*, 77). Dragons have limbs, but Vance can't call them arms, because arms are what humans have, so he calls them "brachs," from the Latin *bracchium*, meaning "arm," and he lets English words like "brachial" suggest a gloss (*DM*). A life support system on an alien space ship sustains life, but to remind the reader of its unearthly origin Vance calls it not a "sustainer" but a "sustenator" (*SOK*, 83). Thus he breathes the aura of alienity into the most familiar objects: an anesthetic without after-effects becomes a "sleep inducent with minimal post reducts" (*StK*, 113).

Vance's words fail in their intended effect if we understand them too well. If we read his 16th-century synonyms or his medical terminology and recognize it for what it is, our response is skewed; we say, "Ah! This character is an antiquarian" or "This character is a doctor"—and we're wrong. These characters are *not of our world*—that is the only thing about them the language is meant to tell us.

We can prove this by noting the one area of the dictionary Vance can't use: contemporary slang. Every other corner of the vocabulary is open to him, but not slang because it is too strongly marked for time, place, and social status. If a character says "rugose" or "brach" or "libram," we only know that he's *not* one of us, but if he calls a policeman "flatfoot," says "rip off" for "steal," calls money "dough," or says "Give me some skin" when he wants to shake hands, we must date, place, and type him. This would be death to Vance's illusion.

At one point in *Life*, Baron Bodissey comments on one of his own vacuous truisms: "This is a large statement, possibly of no startling novelty. Nevertheless, as a generality, it affords a rich resonance of implications" (*StK*, 62). The rich resonance is apparent only to the Baron, but his attitude is a good gloss on reading Vance generally: Vance's world, like the Baron's prose, has a resonance richer than its contents, a resonance we feel but cannot see. The furniture of the world is often mundane enough; yet the resonance remains, created almost entirely by language. Vance frees his words from meaning, so that they can get on with their primary function, the creation of an emotively rich ambiance. Vance's characteristic "subtlety" is often only an impression achieved by cloaking mundane matters in a near-impenetrable fog of redundancy, fractured syntax, vacuous abstraction, and circumlocution—an intentional obscurity.

Sometimes, Vance's skill at making much of little by manipulating language seems a delightful game; sometimes it seems little more than an infuriating pretense of profundity. Exactly where the one becomes the other, perhaps no one can say. Is it delightful or infuriating when Banbeck asks the sacerdotes if they have a weapon to drive off the Basic invaders, and the Elder replies, "Only within the narrow limits of special interpretation"—meaning, "in a sense"? (*DM*, 55). Or when Xanten of Castle Hagedorn has a question answered, and he "sense[s] an adumbration extending yet beyond"—meaning, "he knew there was more to it"? (82). Or when Xanten hears something and "the explicit essense of the revelation failed to strike home into his consciousness"—meaning "he didn't understand"? (85). Sometimes the language has so much slack in it that we must simply import the meaning of entire phrases from context, as when Vance says of hussade that it "assumes an exotic semblance," and apparently means that it's weird (*W*, 221); or when Adam Reith states that the colors of the Tschai natives' clothes "impart a sense of rich essense," and he apparently means they look rich (*CC*, 107). Sometimes, the gap between language surface and transmitted content is so huge that we're left clutching air and wondering where the meaning went, as when Vance describes the world-view of the Djan by saying "Djan cosmology was both supple and subtle; their portents derived as much from caprice as coherent systemology" (*MT*, 10). And would anyone want to defend the double redundancy of "coherent systemology," which means something like "systematic system of systems"?

How one feels about using language to maximize rich resonance in this way will probably determine whether one will treasure Vance or anathematize him, because it is at the heart of his work, and cannot be read around. He is a Demon Prince, seeking to invent forms of emotional intensity heretofore unreached; when he succeeds, it's glorious, and when he goes too far he looks like a bubble-gum blower who didn't know when to stop inflating.

Nor is it a youthful fancy regretted in his maturity; on the contrary, Vance's resonances get richer, his verbal texture thicker, his pumping up of mundane meaning more heavy-handed and fantastic as his career progresses. His later novels use more and more words to say less and less, until they become epics of resonance, with almost nothing underneath the language. And the business of expressing substance in language—the theme of *Pao*—becomes an implicit theme in all of Vance's late work. The novels become more and more ostentatiously made out of language; characters become more consciously lost in language, blinded by it, or armed with it like a weapon.

VANCE'S LISTS

A dozen skills, didactics, and expertises.

Vance's words are as striking in their quantity as in their quality; they come in waves and torrents. Vance likes to enumerate the furniture of his world, and he makes his landscapes seem even busier than they are by naming the same thing several different ways. On one page of the *Dying Earth* he refers to amulets as amulets, periapts, talismans, charms, puissances, thaumaturgical artifacts, instruments, and curiosa (6).

The symbol of Vance's overstuffed worlds is the list. Vance lists everything: when he says the streets are filled with workers, he lists nineteen occupations to prove it (*E*, 55); when he says a scene takes place in a business district, he lists ten kinds of shop (*POL*, 61). These lists often boast of how unnecessary they are by being tacked on to sentences already complete without them, with a colon: in Shagfe "beside the road a dozen crones...huddled beside...goods to be traded: mounds of dark-red meal, thongs of dried meat, blue-black finger grubs in boxes of wet moss, fat greenbeetles tethered to stakes, sugar pods, boiled birds, cardamoms, salt crusts" (*As*, 63). And Vance habitually omits the expected conjunction "and," to suggest that the list goes on, but he has just quit recording it.

Typically Vance's scene descriptions are lists of items: flora (*GP*, 130), fleeting sensory impressions (*TLF*, 12), architectural or geographical components (*DE*, 22; *POL*, 153). One result of this is that Vance's world remains un-put-together for us—we're handed the props, but we must dress the set. A castle is only "a complicated system of towers, turrets, promenades, bays, balconies, and eyries" (*MA*, 76)—assemble them however you will.

Lists can do a number of things. Alfred Bester is a great maker of lists, and for him the list is a symbol of the pathology of his world, representing psychotic hysteria. In Vance, the list never carries this sense; rather, it suggests a prodigal imagination overflowing with riches at every opportunity. When Apollon Zamp loses his showboat crew and advertises for new

57

musicians, Vance jumps at the chance to enumerate the instruments he needs: "Belp-horn, screedle, cadenciver, variboom, elf-pipe, typany, guitar, dulciole, heptagong, zinfonella" (*SW*, 92). No sense of Bester's psychosis; just an imagination happily bursting with invention.

Lists aren't hard to make—you just reach for the Thesaurus and write out a few synonyms for your word—and a few of Vance's lists are made this way, as when he says that traditionally safe conduct has been granted to "wandering minstrels, scholar-poets, bards, scops, druithines, and troubadours" (*SW*, 84); or when Uther Caymon is hanged for being the "accessory, creature, companion, and confidant" of Kokkor Hekkus (*KM*, 156). In each case, the world has only one *thing*, but the verbal surface is enriched four-fold or six-fold by the reduplication.

Vance's lists can be very long—up to fifteen items—but the normal form is the triplet, a quick threesome we hear so often it becomes a familiar Vancean rhythm. "[They] dosed themselves with toners, ameliorators, and antigens" (*E*, 150); "Singhalissa... professed a dozen skills, didactics, and expertises" (*MA*, 161); Interchange is guarded by a "system of alarms, tattletales, and triggerbeams" (*KM*, 90). Occasionally, triplets of triplets: "The Tamarchists engage in wanton violence, destruction, and defilement;...they pollute lakes, reservoirs, and fountains with corpses, filth, and crude oil" (*T*, 127). Vance is by no means merely making lists as long as he can. Such lists are easy to extend: why not, in addition to toners, etc., vaccines, innoculations, boosters, immunizers, and injections?

Usually Vance's lists are not simply synonyms; rather, he divides the concept. He doesn't give us ten words meaning "food"; he distinguishes ten kinds of food. Thus instead of saying "The woodwork was fine hardwood," he says, the "interior stairs, balusters, floors, moldings, and wainscotings were ironwood, pearl sachuli, verbane, Szintarre teak" (*GP*, 60). When Efraim needs to learn the floor plans of his castle, he has them brought to him, and instead of "studying" them, he "traces, retraces, simplifies, codes, and renders [them] comprehensible" (*MA*, 94)—as well he might, since the castle consists of passages "intersecting, opening into nodes, ascending, descending...each overlooking chambers, corridors, and halls through an assortment of peep-holes, periscopes, gratings, and image-amplifiers"! (95).

Vance's desire to load each rift with ore is revealed by a stylistic feature that is the literary equivalent of Hamburger Helper. He likes to end his lists with a vague abstraction that adds the illusion of bulk without adding substance. The Palace of Love, for instance, is "a loose grouping of terraces, halls, and *pleasances*" (154)—the last a Vancean coining suggesting pleasantries that can't be named. The Kruthe language is complex because of "scores of tenses, moods, and *aspects*" (*CC*, 20)—the last meaning nothing more specific than "features." This touch can result in a wonderful crescendo of verbiage, as when Vance describes the smell of "ammonia, ensilage, a dozen sorts of dung, the taint of old meat, *general acridity*" (*EO*, 130); or the human evils from which the demon Blikdak has been brewed: "the sweaty condensation, the stench and vileness, the cloacal humors, the brutal delights, the rapes and sodomies, the scatophilac whims, the manifold tittering lubricities..." (*DE*, 154).

The list nourishes Vance's coinages with an immediate gloss by surrounding them with near-synonyms. Thus Vance's vocabular licentiousness appears most boldly in such lists. Many of the examples we've already quoted contain fine coinages, so a single example here will suffice. When a peddlar offers for sale "drugs, elixirs, wambles, and potions," the other three words gloss the oddball, so we needn't reach for our dictionary to discover to our confusion that "wamble" really means "stomach upset"! (*DE*, 23).

Vance's lists are so eager to add abundance on top of abundance that they break the basic rules of classification: keep the categories parallel and mutually exclusive. Vance's categories overlap, duplicate each other, and leap from one level of abstraction, generalization, or diction to another: for example, if he were to list the parts of the body, he'd list teeth, incisors, and chewing apparatus; legs, limbs, members, and pediments; viscera, innards, and guts. Guyal of Sfere's wonderful Expansible Egg is "impermeable to thew, claw, ensorcelment, pressure, sound, and chill" (*DE*, 112). Our sense of logic is outraged. Claws exert pressure and are often created by ensorcelment, so are these three things or one? Why is the Egg resistant to chill and not heat, to pressure but not puncture, to claw but not fist? When doctors attempt to map Pardero's psychological profile, they chart his "reactions overt, physiological, and cephalic, to absurdities and festivals, erotic conditions, cruelties and horrors, the faces of men, women, and children" (*MA*, 25). This is hardly bearable. Surely physiological reactions are often overt, and surely cephalic reactions are a sub-set of physiological reactions. Absurdity is a pure abstraction, a festival is concrete, and the faces of men are very concrete. The mind reels.

Vance knows the joke in all this, and can play the inconsistency for laughs. A coarse innkeeper offers a sick girl "herbs, sweat-baths, or homeoepathy" (*P*, 83); the scientists of Breakness Institute modify their bodies surgically; Lord Palafox, "one of the most powerfully modified men of Breakness, controls nine sensitivities, four energies, three projections, two nullifications, three lethal emanations," plus four modifications that defy categorization! (*LP*, 45).

At its best, the enumerating style breathes a healthy vigorous plentitude into an ordinary landscape. "I want to buy fiaps [amulets] to protect us from harm" becomes the following Byzantine symphony:

> The sky-car must be protected against every manner of damage, nuisance, and misfortune, including pilferage, destruction, curiosity, tampering, vandalism, defilement, removal, or concealment. I want fiaps for myself

and my companions, guarding us against molestation, harm, magic, beguilement, exploitation, capture, or immobility, and the various stages and conditions of death (*GP*, 87).

Vance is like a host who serves simple fare and calls each dish by an elegant French name. We dine like gourmets, eating with our ears and not our mouths.

Making distinctions between kinds of things is central to Vance's art. As he says in the "Forward" to *Eight Fantasms and Magics*, "The range of events is wide and only roughly amenable to classification" (7)—but he will try. Vance's world is full of people who strive to order experience by classifying it. The Rac torturers have reduced the science of pain to eleven maximally efficacious "programs" of torment (*NP*, 199), and most of Vance's people share the Racs' urge to order things in this way. So does Vance: he bases his finest work, the Demon Prince series, on just such a division of an abstraction. Each of the five Demon Princes, we are constantly reminded, is an artist of terror, but each finds his own personal style, his own kind of terror. Distinguishing between one sort of supreme villainy and another often looks like trying to cut a glass of water into slices with a sharp knife; but a quotation from the fictitious volume *Demon Princes* explains the rationale: the author, Caril Carphen, says the Princes have trouble remaining distinct, because "the basic variety of possible crimes is limited and can be numbered on the fingers," which Carphen proceeds to do ("The personal depravities are equally limited, and can be classified under sexual debauchery," etc.). He concludes, "Doubtless the catalogue is incomplete, perhaps even illogical, but this is beside the point. I merely wish to display the basic paucity, in order to illustrate this point: that each of the Demon Princes, in inflicting one or another atrocity, impresses the act with his own style and seems to create a new crime" (*StK*, 122). Carphen is describing Vance's illusion of alien uniqueness exactly. The varieties of intense emotion are finite, all exploited long ago. To make something appear unique and new, Vance, the king of all Demon Princes, invests the old thing with the aura of newness through personal style, through dividing the old concepts into distinct categories that exist only in language.

LATINISMS AND NOMINALIZATIONS

An insufficiency of Termagants.

Vance's style habitually chooses words derived from Latin, and transforms phrases that are naturally verbal or adjectival into nouns. The two methods work together, so that in each of the following phrases, the unnatural nominalization is also a weighty latinate word.

"He brought an insufficiency of Termagants" (*DM*, 38) [He didn't bring enough Termagants]: "I am at a loss for decision" (*EO*, 12) [I can't decide]: "Allow me at least a contravention" (*T*, 130) [Let me disagree]: "He essayed conversation" (*W*, 143) [He tried talking]: One "perceived an incorrectness" (*As*, 183) [He saw something was wrong]: "From below came the sounds of ingress" (*As*, 130) [He heard someone coming in]: and the habitual "I admit to curiosity/perplexity/diffidence, etc." (*MT*, 206; *P*, 86; *T*, 123, etc.).

Latinate words are abstract, difficult, long, chilling. Nominalization is impersonal, unnatural, and academic. The overall effect of the two together is to distance us from the text, to remove the personality, the color, the sensuality from the language, and make it formal and reserved. We know this language—we recognize it as the language of unreadable textbooks, stuffy lectures, Pentagon news conferences, stonewalling politicians. Such language turns the human "Crime is on the rise again, and I'm worried" into the sanitized "The recent resurgence in criminal activities is a source of concern." Vance seeks this kind of damping of energy: his people speak of effecting "regeneracy" when they mean terrifying a population into obedience (*W*, 199); speak of "the accommodation of one's daughter" when they mean having sex with her (*T*, 86); speak of "inanition" instead of "hunger" (*P*, 21); speak of "acrimony" instead of "rage" (*SW*, 66). When a villain delivers a good man into the hands of his enemies for cash he is guilty of nothing more graspable than "inordinacy" (*D*, 146). In such a style, the actors disappear, and their acts or qualities become the nominalized center of attention: "Somewhere in his mind cogitation occurred," Vance says, meaning, "He thought" (*An*, 28); Etzwane makes official decrees and sends out representatives to "note particulars of recalcitrance," meaning punish anyone who disobeys (*BFM*, 45).

THE REALITY MAP, PART II

With luck we should be able
to strike a fix upon our subject.

What do these features suggest about the shape of the world Vance wants us to perceive? Much of what we've said in the last pages seems to contradict what we said before about Vance's joyful prodigality. Before, he seemed spendthrift, sensual, intense; now he seems clinical, neutral, abstract. Which is he? Both. Arthur Jean Cox and Richard Tiedman have both noted Vance's abstract/sensuous paradox (*JV*, 184-5), but haven't accounted for it. The clinical style is the medium by which Vance's characters perceive and interact with a sensuous world. Characters use the style to organize, sterilize, and euphemize a world of otherwise unbearable emotional intensity. The language Vance's people use to characterize their world is purposefully inappropriate; Vance intentionally exaggerates the gap between map and reality, between verbal surface and subtext. His characters do it too—intentionally, if they are enlightened, or unconsciously, if self-deceived. In a word, Vance sees the world *ironically*, and Vance's characters, intentionally or not, are ironists.

Vance uses the abstract style to characterize alien races whose conceptual categories aren't human, as in the dialogue between Joaz Banbeck and an emissary from the alien Basics: when Banbeck asks, "What is your message?," the Basic replies, "I bring an integration from my masters," and the conversation goes from bad to worse (*DM*, 83). It also characterizes human races who have abandoned their humanity for one reason or another, like the Pnumekin, who strive to be as much like their Pnume masters as possible, and say "The item made evasion" when Reith escapes (*P*, 23). This euphemistic style characterizes super-sophisticated cultures, where a similar denial of the blood has taken place. When Jubal Droad is set upon by thugs hired by Mieltrude to torture him to death, he expresses his outrage to her father, who translates it into polite terms for her: "He claims to have suffered inconvenience; he begs to place one or two perplexities before you, that you may elucidate the facts to his understanding" (*MT*, 83). Such cultures use the style to deny emotions too intense to be faced: Cath calls its public torturers Ministrants (*SOW*, 79); Sarkovy calls public execution Cooperation (*POL*, 11); Amboy calls antisocial behavior Inclination (*E*, 35). If a citizen of Amboy "inclines" too much, he is subject to Explusion: deviants are "expelled" across the border into the neighboring region of Bauredel; the only problem is that Amboy officials have erected a stone wall one inch over the border and encourage the deviant with a powerful piston behind, so he is invited to enter (in Vance's wonderful phrase) "that single inch of Bauredel territory available for his occupany" (181).

But in the large view, ironic mismatching of language to event is the style of all of Vance's people, the way they endure a world of misfortune, hypocrisy, pain, and horror. No one else in SF has a vision as profoundly humorous as Vance; and that humor is a sardonic, grim-lipped bemusement that exactly fits Heinlein's definition of laughter in *Stranger in a Strange Land*: the human spirit triumphing over a world that is wrong, false, full of misery and fear (Putnam, 1961, 295 ff.).

In Vance's world, horror and misfortune are basically hilarious. Guyal of Sfere defeats the demon Blikdak by attaching him to a high-speed bobbin and unravelling him (*DE*). Malagate kidnaps the mayor of Desde and tortures him for thirty-nine days, telecasting the events to the entire Rigel Concourse (*StK*, 123). In such a world, the true humorists are those who can invent the quaintest torments: Lens Larque is a "prankster," and Howard Alan Treesong's crimes are always Big Jokes. "A more resourceful set of humorists" than the Blue Chasch "has never been known" (*CC*,

118); their idea of wit?—to pen a man in a vat of slime with a valve (located at the bottom so the victim must dive repeatedly to switch it) that either makes the muck boiling or freezing. Iucounu the Laughing Magician is also a card. Cugel asks Zaraides the mage to arm him to defeat Iucounu, and Zaraides replies, "I do not care to pass [my] last hours exchanging jests with Iucounu, whose humor is much more elaborate than my own" (*EO*, 161). Typical of Iucounu's humor is the talisman he gives to Cugel before sending him to the ends of the earth seeking treasure: the amulet will turn anything into "nutriment"; Cugel need never starve. Yet, when he puts it to the test on a piece of driftwood, Cugel finds that instead of transforming the wood into meat, it merely softens it to a point where it may be ingested. But it retains the flavor of driftwood (15).

In a world of such humors, survival depends on being a humorist oneself. Ifness says, "With luck we should be able to strike a fix upon our subject"; "And what if we are unlucky?" responds Etzwane; Ifness replies, "This, to be frank, is my expectation" (*An*, 168). This tone is a defense against a world of woes, an intentional mismatch between the miserable fact and the human representation of it in language.

In Vance, the more ignoble the subject matter, the more inappropriately grandiloquent the language used by people to deal with it. When Gersen visits Tintle's Shade, purveyors of unspeakably vile Darsh food, unspeakably gross Darsh entertainment, and unspeakably rude Darsh women, Gersen's language suggests that the food is epicurean, the entertainment fine art, and the women duchesses (*F*, 26 ff). The Darsh are not persuaded, but Gersen asserts his mastery of his perceived world in this way. When Sarajano escapes from his room, the only exit seems to be a narrow flight of stairs supposedly guarded by Mielke. Frolitz reasons, "Here sat Mielke, on these selfsame stairs, discussing affairs with an undermaid. Agreed: they were not alert to the possibility of Sarajano stepping upon them on his way to freedom; still the occasion seems remote" (*BFM*, 118). This is tact personified: the discussion of affairs, of course, was a sexual tumble, but Frolitz makes it sound like a summit meeting. The low immediacy of "Sarajano stepping upon them" twinkles in the midst of the statement to indicate that Frolitz euphemizes out of wisdom, not blindness.

Vance's world is a world of artists, used car salesmen, and hypocrites, all of whom deal with the world in false language and must be dealt with in kind. When the despicable Woudiver demands payment up front for his services, Reith replies, "All very well. But, as a ridiculous supposition, let us assume that, rather than a man of honor, you were a scoundrel, a knave, a cheat" (*D*, 109)—which of course Woudiver is. Reith does not pay. When Ifness and Etzwane stop at a shady inn for the night, Ifness arranges with the innkeeper to have their boat guarded during the night. Ifness reports, "The innkeeper declares that we might leave ten treasure chests aboard our boat without fear of molestation. He accepts full responsibility, and the risk is thereby reduced. Nevertheless, I will arrange a warning device to discourage those pilferers who might escape his vigilance" (*As*, 50). Ifness knows that telling the innkeeper the boat needs guarding guarantees that the innkeeper will try to plunder it, and indeed the innkeeper is caught in Ifness's alarm system that night.

The more ghastly the reality, the more Vance's people need the distance of irony. Robert Silverberg speaks wisely of "the unfailing courtliness with which [Vance's] murderous beings... address each other" (*JV*, 126 ff). A character says of a slavering demon lurking outside his doors, "Several of my associates have had cause to complain; in fact, all are dead by its odious acts" (*EO*, 45).

This is a cosmos full of truly sickening deeds: babies are torn to pieces (*An*, 130); nice people have their fingers' ends smashed with mallets and are blinded by acid thrown in the face (*W*, 187), or are hung for days by a rod through the cheeks (*KM*, 149), or are flayed inch by inch and then bound in a bag with scorpions (*DE*, 138). Vance's heroes are regularly subjected to expert torture for extended periods of time (*NP*, *FGB*). Yet Vance's horrors are never harrowing, because he and his characters refuse to grant them their due. As Cugal is about to kill a deodand who sought to kill and eat him, they hold the following philosophical discussion:

> "Hold your stroke. You gain nothing by my death."
> "Only the satisfaction of killing one who planned to devour me."
> "A sterile pleasure!"
> "Few pleasures are otherwise" (*EO*, 67).

When Gersen tells Malagate that he plans to kill him, Malagate replies, "You are an ambitious man" (*StK*, 151); when Traz tells Reith that offworlders are routinely killed, Reith replies, "That seems overly harsh" (*CC*, 22). When Lens Larque kidnaps a reporter who wrote a nosy article about the origin of "Panak," Larque's name for his whip, the following letter is received by an associate of the reporter's:

> Dear Cloebe: I am hard at work elucidating the meaning of the name Panak. Already I have discovered several clues, but the work is not without its little surprises. The weather is fine; still I would as lief be home. In all sincerity, Erasmus.

Gersen's informant says in response to this, "The skin tingles a bit, does it not?" (*F*, 20). Indeed it does, but the thrill comes from the refusal of the language to do more than glance at the atrocious reality.

Vance makes torture sound like a tea party, and incalculable depravity is called nothing worse than "noisome." Hildemar Dasce was once disfigured by Robin Rampold; Dasce seized Rampold and transported him to an uninhabited ball of rock in space, where he has lived ever since. Suthiro tells us, "Occasionally Hildemar, remembering the outrage that cost him his features, returns to this private place to *remonstrate* with the man" (*StK*, 96). Rampold is rescued by Gersen and ends up holding Dasce captive; he says at the end of the novel, "Daily I demonstrate to Hildemar Dasce the *tricks* and *conceits* he taught me long ago" (157).

Vance's literary worlds, then, find their unique energy in a dissonant counterpoint between extreme, super-abundant emotion, passion, and sensuousness, and a language that refuses to reflect that intensity. A final example of the Vancean dissonance: on Trullion, the citizens dread the prutanshyr, the state instrument of execution. Vance mentions it often, but only describes its working once and glancingly, when his protagonist catches sight of one: "At the center [of the square] stood the prutanshyr, with its glass cauldron, through the sides of which a criminal being boiled and the rapt crowd might inspect each other" (187). In this sublimely, hideously inappropriate mix of style and subject matter lies the core of Vance's world, and a message about the way human beings use humor to survive in it.

IV
VANCE'S PLOTS

The chain of events is expedited by chance.

Science fiction is inherently plot-centered, because plot, the shaping of events into a purposeful and determined pattern by cause and effect is the literary expression of the scientific relationship to experience. The scientist assumes that the law of cause and effect will hold—events are the regular product of their causes, and are in turn the logical causes of other consequences—and that materials (characters) have inherent properties (personality) and can only act in accordance with them. Thus experience is linear, an event is truly understood in terms of what causes it and what it causes, and the meaning of experience is firmly rooted in Outcome.

A good plot is a reaffirmation of the scientist's rational empiricism, a successful lab experiment in human behavior. Here, outcomes are revealed to be the inevitable result of elements acting according to their natures, and dramatically appropriate conclusions are the logical results of an original impetus.

The virtues of a good plot have been sung since Aristotle, but the architectonic plot was not seen as a central criterion of literary excellence until the age of science, when it flowered in the Augustan novels of Fielding and Austen. Since the eighteenth century, the notion of plot as the cornerstone of the literary work has grown with the growing acceptance of the scientific metaphor for experience, until its ultimate expression in the detective novel of the nineteenth and twentieth centuries, in which all that matters is the cause-and-effect relationship between events, and where a character is powerful only insofar as he is able to divine this relationship—the Sherlock Holmes myth.

The bond between detective fiction and science fiction has always been strong—traditionally SF-oriented writers and editors have often been successful in the other field as well—because SF shares the detective story's values, but takes them one step further: whereas Holmes assumes that the scientific method can reveal the meaning of any earthly human experience, SF assumes the method will obtain for all races, all situations, on Earth or orbiting distant stars.

A good SF writer, then, it would seem, must plot well. Jack Vance does not plot well—his works often *appear* to be plot-centered, but aren't. Though there are enough exceptions to prove that he can plot well when he wants to, and his plotting in his detective fiction (published under the name John Holbrook

Vance) proves his skill in this area, in most of his SF he avoids such obligations whenever possible, plotting casually or badly, and finally turning away from plot altogether in his later works, finding it a distraction from more static things of real value. The late novels are almost wholly plotless: dramatic action seems ignored, trumped up, gone through halfheartedly by an author whose spirit is in other aspects of the work; it is also often summarily aborted, to the plot-oriented reader's rage. And as the plots get thinner, the verbal texture gets thicker, the cultural surface of Vance's alien worlds becomes denser and more emotionally resonant. Finally, unlike hard SF, which sings the praises of the linear man, who lives for Outcome—which glorifies him—Vance's fiction documents his folly.

Throughout most of his career, Vance has had the look of the classic SF plotter. His early protagonists are supremely rational empiricists: For example, his first hero, Magnus Ridolph, space trouble-shooter and private eye; Kirth Gersen of the Demon Princes series; Adam Reith of the Tschai tetralogy; Sklar Hast of *The Blue World*; Joaz Banbeck of *The Dragon Masters*; and others are all logical problem-solvers. Nearly all of Vance's plots center around classic exercises in problem-solving and logistics: solving crimes, locating, identifying, and capturing criminals, waging military battles, engineering social revolutions, escaping from imprisonment, avoiding capture, building sophisticated machines (spaceships and such) in primitive cultures or under enormous handicaps, stealing heavily guarded treasures, or deducing and exploiting the customs and mores of unfamiliar societies. For instance:

> In *The Five Gold Bands*, Paddy Blackthorn comes to possess five bracelets, each containing the location of the hiding place of one-fifth of the mathematics of space drive, a secret kept from Earthmen by five alien races. His mission: decipher the instructions on the five bracelets, penetrate five complex, unfamiliar, and suspicious societies, and sneak the information back to Earth against the efforts of the combined police forces of the Galaxy.

> In *The Dragon Masters*, Joaz Banbeck must defeat his hostile neighbor Ervis Carcolo in battle through superior military tactics, then defeat the forces of the Basics, alien space depredators bent on enslaving Banbeck's people and armed with vastly superior weaponry. This he does by deducing that the sacerdotes, mysterious autochthons dwelling underground, must know how to defeat the Basics; and then maneuvering the battle to ensure that the Basic attack threatens the sacerdotes' sacred places, forcing them to destroy the Basics for him.

> In each of the Demon Prince novels, protagonist Kirth

Gersen plays space private eye, locating and destroying one faceless, mighty galactic villain after another. Always the search involves Gersen in problems of deduction: in *The Star King* and *The Palace of Love*, he knows the villain to be one of three suspects, and must establish his identity beyond doubt from circumstantial evidence; in *The Star King* and *The Killing Machine*, he must deduce the location of a planet from apparently unrelated scraps of information—nursery rhymes, old travel itineraries, the physical properties of mechanical devices from the planet, and the like.

In *The Blue World*, Sklar Hast and his people live on large rafts of living vegetation called floats in a watery world on which their spacecraft crashed generations earlier. In this world, offering nothing beyond fish carcasses, water, and vegetable fiber for raw materials, Hast develops an electricity-and-iron technology capable of destroying the kragen, armor-plated aquatic behemoths that tyrannize and despoil the floats.

In *The Houses of Iszm*, Earth botanist Aile Farr is unknowingly used as a pawn in a plot to steal the most carefully guarded prize in the galaxy: a seed of an Iszm treehouse.

In *Big Planet*, the Tschai tetralogy, "The New Prime" and other places, Vance's protagonists find themselves set down in alien cultures they know nothing about, and are asked to cope, to survive, and usually build transportation home despite barbaric surroundings or advanced races who are trying to capture and destroy them.

Since all of Vance's books focus on actions like these, how can we say that plot is not central to Vance's world?

For one thing, Vance frees himself from an obligation to plot at all, by using structures of action and plot devices that make cause-and-effect sequences irrelevant or impossible. He likes the picaresque plot, for instance, in which the protagonist is given the task of getting from a geographical starting place across hostile or unknown territory to a home base, a place of safety. The plot is then merely a series of unconnected episodes, sausages on a string that is the road. This is the basic structure of *Big Planet*, *The Eyes of the Overworld*, *Showboat World*, *Space Opera*, the Tschai tetralogy, and large portions of other works, like the Durdane trilogy. In *Big Planet*, for instance, the Earth delegation to Big Planet is sabotaged before it lands; it crashes, and the rest of the novel chronicles the delegation's trek through a series of striking cultural enclaves, each posing its problem in first contact or survival. In *The*

Eyes of the Overworld, Cugel the Clever rashly tries to rob the manse of Iucounu the Laughing Magician. Iucounu traps him, and in punishment transports him to a far corner of the globe to find and bring back an Eye of the Overworld. Cugel soon gets the eye, and spends the rest of the novel wending his way from one eccentric tribe or village to the next.

Picaresque novels need not be composed of unrelated episodes (after all, much of *Tom Jones*, the ultimate architectonic novel, is picaresque), but Vance's are almost entirely so. The unconnectedness suits Vance's taste perfectly, since he delights in striking off dazzling portraits of cultural eccentricity in miniature, and has by nature none of *Dune*'s fascination with the interplay of multiple cultural perspectives. Herbert likes to play Bene Gesserit pranabindu training *against* Guild prescience *against* Fremen cunning, but Vance prefers to have a neutral, competent, unjudgmental outsider encounter the worldviews in series, with each encounter complete at once, each problem solved, each lesson learned, and each village forgotten at the next bend in the road. Typically at the end of a Vancean episode, all ties with the past are broken, and the protagonist proceeds to a virgin game board, a brand new game, and a new set of rules just over the ridge.

Vance justifies the unconnectedness with a simple fictional premise. On Big Planet, we are told, metal is so scarce that the technology for planetary communications has never developed; thus each cultural pocket is cut off from its neighbors and is excused from knowing what has happened in the previous chapter. In the Tschai tetralogy, in which Adam Reith, Earth explorer scout, is shot down over the planet Tschai and left to wend his way through four volumes of idiosyncratic cultures, seeking a ride back to Earth, Vance postulates that all the races and tribes of Tschai hate and distrust each other and hold themselves strictly aloof from each other's business—thus, when Reith leaves Cath, Vance is able to assume that wherever he goes next will have no contact with Cath, and so Reith's adventures in Cath will make no plot ripples elsewhere.

Since Vance's picaresque frames free him from any obligation to provide causal connections between events in series, these novels can end at any time—or never end. The protagonist travels the road until Vance tires of inventing encounters, whereupon he provides him with a more or less convincing ride home. At the end of *Big Planet*, Claude Glystra, the protagonist, stumbles into a way home that is as likely on the first step of his journey as it is on the last.

We become so comfortable with Vance's unconnectedness that his occasional flashes of plot—where we suddenly realize that he's been looking forward or backward—catch us unawares. In the first volume of the Tschai series, Reith meets the Emblemmen, who wear ancient medallions handed down through generations, and assume the personality of the emblems they inherit. Reith is befriended by Traz, who wears Onmale, courageous leader of the tribe. When Traz accompanies Reith on his journey, Reith buries

Onmale in the ground (*CC*, 40). Onmale is forgotten for two and one-half volumes, but he is not dead, and in volume three, Reith suddenly and convincingly calls him forth from Traz's unconscious to save them from the pursuing Dirdir hunters (*D*, 75). We are dazzled; having forgotten that in most science fiction novels actions inevitably result in later consequences (or reactions), we feel that Vance is almost cheating to plan ahead like this, and we are delighted at the novelty.

Similarly, we recognize that, while Vance typically begins his novels with an emphatic dramatic push forward—a problem demanding solution, a goal that must be attained for safety's sake, and so on—the push is often *pro forma*, an excuse to get on with the business of encountering one alien culture after another. The push is often lost sight of—and we don't mind—and occasionally dispatched with pitiless indifference midway through the action. Once the protagonist is rolling along the road, we needn't nurture the fiction that got him going. For example, the Tschai tetralogy begins with a mystery that Reith sets out to solve: who shot him down with a missile as he approached Tschai and began to reconnoitre? Few of the races on Tschai have the technology, and none apparently has the interest. This gives Reith a direction, but he is immediately swept up in his first cultural encounter, with the savage and beautiful Emblemmen, and the mystery is thereafter only dusted off occasionally as rationale for forcing Reith to interact with every major culture on the planet. The mystery is quietly solved, not at the end of the series but midway through, and I suspect that most readers shared my dismay when I finished the series and found myself still asking, "Who *did* shoot him down, anyway?" The "mystery" is revealed near the end of the second volume, when Reith is giving a speech to the Wankh about more important matters. The Wankhmen, the human servants of the Wankh, did it, for flimsy reasons. Dependent on the Wankh, they have been systematically destroying everything that might upset the ancient war between the Wankh and the Dirdir, and thus end the Wankh's need for them. The rationale hardly matters, however, and the novels proceed smoothly forward even if one reads past it.

And Vance does not always wait until the halfway mark to end the pretense of forward momentum: In *Marune*, the initial mystery concerns the identity of an amnesiac who materializes one day at Carfaunge Airport. His psychological profile indicates an origin on the planet Marune, so he goes there. But how to find his identity and his past amidst the bustle of a populous, unfamiliar planet, and an extremely subtle, treacherous cultural mind-set? He checks into a hotel, and is instantly recognized by the desk clerk—problem solved (*MA*, 54).

Vance is also fond of destroying the cause-and-effect sequencing of events with a *deus ex machina*, the agent of supreme power who appears out of the air to solve dramatic problems that cannot be solved internally, as a consequence of ongoing action. In the Durdane series, the *deus* is Ifness, representative of Earth's Historical Institute on the world of Durdane. As Gastel

Etzwane, native of Durdane and the series' protagonist, strives to locate the Anome, the Faceless Man who directs the world's social order, and to solve the mysteries that surround him, Ifness is a companion of infinite potential. We don't know what he's after, and he has access to Earth's limitless knowledge; thus Vance can have him do anything the plot requires—he's a dramatic *carte blanche*. If Etzwane needs information, Ifness will happen to possess it; if Etzwane is in danger, Ifness will happen to know of it and have the means to save him; if Etzwane lacks motivation to do something, Ifness can talk him into doing it. Ifness is the equivalent of Batman's utility belt: whenever the events of the day necessitate a particular tool, you can be sure Batman happened to pack it that morning. Ifness can do anything, and so Vance is saved from all the logistical problems of tight plotting.

In his last group of novels, the Alastor books, which all take place on planets in the Alastor Cluster, Vance embraces the luxury of the *deus ex machina* openly. He tells us at the beginning of each novel that a benevolent and omnipotent god overlooks the Cluster and guarantees justice in the last chapter. He is the Connatic, the supreme ruler of the Cluster, who wanders the Cluster incognito, righting wrongs at the eleventh hour. At the end of *Wyst*, for instance, when the momentum of events seems to be lost and the protagonist has wandered far from the plot and is stagnating in a backwater, the Connatic appears and simply assigns just desserts.

Vance's favorite *deus ex machina* is the Fully Informed Stranger. When the protagonist needs to know something in order to advance, and the information cannot be plausibly revealed by the probable actions of the characters in the drama, Vance simply has the protagonist run into a stranger who knows everything the protagonist needs to be told. Ifness does this for Etzwane: at the end of *The Brave Free Men*, when Etzwane has been trying for two volumes with no success to discover the secret of the Rogushkoi, the alien hordes depredating Durdane's countryside, Ifness informs him that while Etzwane has been playing hero in battle against the beasts, Ifness has been quietly getting answers in the dissection lab, and we get six pages of exposition from Ifness—all the answers to all the dramatic questions that plot has raised, but failed to answer. Similarly, in *Emphyrio*, the protagonist Ghyl Tarvoke devotes his life to seeking the answers to the questions: Who was Emphyrio? Is his legend true? What happened to him in the end? Ghyl wanders through his culture seeking answers and getting nowhere; finally he goes to Earth, where Rolus, representative of the Historical Institute, simply punches buttons on the computer, and all the answers are spat forth from the memory bank.

Again and again, Vance's protagonists' guests go nowhere, until they ask the Fully Informed Stranger to do the plot's task, and matters are handled in pages of expository discourse by the voice of authority—a computer, a representative of an august body of encyclopedists, or an omniscient Connatic.

This convenient lever to free a stuck plot shows clearly in Vance's most finely plotted works: *The Killing Machine*, for instance, probably Vance's best plot. In this volume in the Demon Prince series, Gersen sets out to locate and destroy Kokkor Hekkus, the Killing Machine, a horrific legend hidden in a galaxy of countless billions of trackless souls. Where to begin? Gersen has information that suggests that one "Billy Windle" is a confederate of Hekkus's, and he suspects that Windle might in fact be Hekkus. On an out-of-the-way planet, waiting for Windle, Gersen hires a tavern boy to run errands for him and, just to pass the time, the boy casually volunteers the information that Billy Windle is a hormagaunt (a vampire of souls) who lives on Thamber (*KM*, 15). Thus in the opening pages of the action, a nobody hands Gersen, for no reason, the two secrets at the heart of the novel; secrets, the rest of the novel implies, known to no one in the universe except Hekkus and this tavern boy.

But Gersen needs more help. Windle escapes, and Thamber's location is a mystery, so Gersen needs a new lead. "The chain of events [is] expedited by chance," Vance is frank enough to admit. Gersen is sitting idly on a park bench when a stranger sharing the bench engages him in conversation about the laxity of current law enforcement. Why, just the other day, the stranger volunteers, he saw "an associate of the notorious Kokkor Hekkus" walking in the direction of Sailmaker Beach! (*KM*, 21) Since no one in the galaxy is supposed to know who works for Hekkus, Gersen naturally asks how the stranger knows. It seems that the stranger years earlier witnessed a trial in which the defendent got off, and it was rumored that Hekkus tampered with the jury. The stranger never forgot the defendent's face, and saw it again in the street recently. Could he describe the man? Of course, in great detail.

At its most powerful, the *deus ex machina* can even violate the laws of Vance's own cosmos, making plots that refuse to progress consequentially finally come to some conclusion. In *Marune*, the protagonist Efraim has lost his memory from a dose of a memory-destroying drug of the Fwai-chi, a sort of herbal-medicine tribe of autochthones. Unless he can recover his memory, he will never know who drugged him, shanghaied him, and committed a list of other crimes—murder, theft of birthright, and so on. Can the memory be recovered? Absolutely not, say the Fwai-chi: "The poison breaks the roads to the memory tablets. These roads will never mend" (*MA*, 126). The matter is closed—or is it? At the end of the novel, the Fwai-chi change their metaphor: "Your memory is locked and there are no keys to the locks...We cannot unlock the doors; but we can batter them open" (*MA*, 158). A drug is administered, and the memory recovered. Vance may claim that he resolves his dramatic problems with "pure deduction in the classical pattern" (*BD*, 8), but he's wrong.

The picaresque format and the liberal use of the *deus ex machina* are ways Vance excuses himself from the responsibility of linear, cause-and-effect plotting. When he does plot, his plots are riddled with anti-climaxes, improbable premises, red herrings, flukey resolutions, and aborted dramatic actions. These apparent problems increase as Vance's career advances, until we get to the late works, *Maske: Thaery*, *Trullion: Alastor 2262*, *Wyst: Alastor 1716*, and *Marune: Alastor 993*, which are all plotting fiascos.

Wyst's mystery is based on a premise of hallucinatory improbability: a group of the protagonist Jantiff's smarmy friends happen to look just like the Whispers, the ruling Elder council of the planet Wyst, so they decide to kill the Whispers and take their places—something akin to you and your friends happening to notice that you look just like Ronald Reagan and his cabinet and so deciding to take their places. Jantiff finds this plot so unappealing that he leaves in the midst of it and escapes to the wild seashore, where he spends his days gathering percels (local oysters) and living in a shack with a witch girl who never speaks. He and the reader are much happier there—he says that there he's "truly alive" for the first time, and we believe him (*W*, 201)—and he is recalled somewhat reluctantly by the Connatic to finish the obligatory plot.

Maske, a tissue of loose ends and questions unanswered (for instance, we're never told who murdered protagonist Jubal Droad's father), ends with one of the great anti-climaxes in literature. Jubal spends the novel pursuing arch-villain Ramus Ymph—dashing, brooding, unscrupulous, malevolent—and trying to figure out what diabolical scheme the twisted lordling is incubating, to the everlasting woe of the planet Maske. Jubal runs Ymph to ground, and discovers that Ymph plans to...set up a travel agency and open Maske to tourism! The depth of Ymph's perfidy is no surprise, since he has already been discovered smuggling native rugwork. Shades of Retief!

Trullion is a novel in search of a dramatic pull that will last long enough to get us to the conclusion. A long list of dramatic actions are begun with high hopes, but each in turn dies aborning, resolving itself too soon, or wandering off in disinterest. The protagonist Glinnes returns home to his ancestral home on the Everglade-like world of Trullion to find a number of problems on his hands: his father is dead, and his twin brother Glay, a hot-headed vagabond, has illegally sold Ambal Isle, a part of the family estate, to a stranger, who now won't leave. To void the sale, Glinnes must buy back the land or prove he's the heir, but his elder brother has disappeared and Glinnes can't prove he's dead. Glinnes unwisely loves Dissane, the daughter of a gypsy named Vang Drosset who hates Glinnes; Drosset robs Glinnes of the money Glinnes plans to buy back the family lands with; and the entire culture that Glinnes loves is threatened by fanscherade, an ill-considered movement for social reform and trendy destruction of the old values among the culture's fretful youth. Surely this is enough stuff to make a plot out of. Yet one by one these veins of plot peter out: Glay becomes caught up in fanscherade and loses interest in his bid for the estate; Dissane decides to marry a rich boor from a neighboring island, and Glinnes realizes it's just as well; Glinnes simply steals back the money Drosset stole from him; to prove he is the true heir, Glinnes simply beats up the murderer of his brother, threatens him with death and forces him to confess; the colony of fanschers foolishly settles on the sacred land of the savage Trevanyi, who slaughter them for trespass, and fanscherade is suddenly a thing of the past. Two-thirds of the way through, the novel is dead in the water, all dramatic impetus spent. Glinnes, like most of Vance's late protagonists, wisely absents himself from the plot as much as possible, and spends most of the book playing hussade (a cross between football and water polo).

Finally, a new mystery offers itself. Space pirates kidnap an entire stadium of spectators at a prestigious hussade match; a ransom is demanded and collected, but it disappears before it can be delivered. Glinnes is implicated. The culprit, the despicable, pompous nobleman Gensifer, is finally found out, but his guilt is revealed by his own incomprehensibly idiotic blunder: when he made contact with the pirates, he masked himself to preserve his identity, but chose to wear the distinctive helmet of his hussade team to do so. Since the helmets are unique to the team, unforgettably striking in appearance, and were brand new, so that only Gensifer, the team's owner, as yet had access to them, Gensifer was advertising his identity with neon signs and fireworks. Why would he do such a thing? To get to the end of the book, we must assume.

With a rare exception like *The Blue World*, all of Vance's novels either are single long episodes (*The Last Castle*), avoid the responsibilities of plotting through devices like the picaresque structure, or sport plotting weaknesses such as those described above. Yet the poorness of the plots is not Vance's failure, but rather his message to us that plot is not the thing that matters in his fiction. In *The Star King*, Marmaduke in "The Avatar's Apprentice" is reprimanded by the wise Eminence for missing the Eminence's point during a lesson. "The way along the Parapet is not to the forward-footed," the Eminence admonishes (*StK*, 142). The forward-footed reader, he who assumes that the purpose of fiction is to move ahead to Outcome, has like Marmaduke missed the point, and Vance will educate him to a new orientation. The linear reader learns what Vance's heroes repeatedly learn: that living linearly always proves to be a sham. Plots abort, or are maintained by sleight-of-hand, or prove barren in completion—this is life's failure, Vance says, not his.

Vance's career begins with a strong linear surface, but by the 1970s the superior value of static things can be openly acknowledged. The shift is visible in his titles (although this also reflects a corresponding shift in the values of SF publishing). The early novels' titles are the goals their linear heroes seek—treasures to steal, villains to destroy, great deeds to do: *The Five Gold Bands*, *Son of the Tree*, *The Star King*, *To Live Forever*. The late novels tend to locate their centers of value in places, cultural ambiances, textures, social structures and customs, and so their titles are the environments in which the action—or inaction—takes place: Trullion, Maske, Showboat World,

Wyst, Marune.

There is a similar change in the character of the Vancean protagonist. Vance's early books, as we have said, are headed by classic SF rational empiricists, trained reasoners and copers in the Campbell-Asimov tradition, bristling with left-brain skills often honed by years of disciplined training—Adam Reith, for instance:

> He had assimilated vast quantities of basic sciences, linguistic and communication theory, astronautics, space and energy technology, biometrics, meteorology, geology, toxicology. So much was theory; additionally he had been trained in practical survival techniques of every description: weaponry, attack and defense, emergency nutrition, rigging and hoisting, space-drive mechanics, electronic repair, and improvisation (*CC*, 18).

These men burn with a consuming need to get "There." Joaz Banbeck of *The Dragon Masters* burns to escape the planet and reestablish contact with the lost race of men; Guyal of Sfere in *The Dying Earth* aches to know the reason for Man's existence and to rekindle the race's dying frontier spirit—and so on.

With *Emphyrio*, Vance perfects a new kind of protagonist. Ghyl Tarvoke, and Vance's other mid-career protagonists, are right-brain affectives/intuitives. They lack all training in rational skills, and are not outsiders invading a culture and dominating it with extracultural expertise; instead, they are ordinary members of their hand-work cultures—woodworkers, farmers, and such—distinguished only by a kind of fatedness, a destiny more akin to Tarot than explorer training. Tarvoke is called "fey" by Holkerwoyd the puppetmaster, meaning fated, pregnant with destiny, doomed, even anointed. This new protagonist is quiet, listless, without apparent talent of any sort, separated from his fellows only by a quiet sense of discontent, a vague urging to do something he can't define. He meanders into dramatic actions, allowing himself to drift with destiny; the plot seems almost to happen to him. These men topple entire social systems, but do so almost by the way, aghast at their own presumption and at the role destiny has asked them to play.

In Vance's last works, a third kind of protagonist emerges. Even less linear than Tarvoke, he feels no urge to do anything. Tarvoke hears a voice within him that calls him to quest—he just can't figure out what to seek. He would go There if he knew where There was. But the protagonists of *Trullion*, *Maske*, and *Wyst* just want to stay home or pursue a simple vocation. Glinnes of *Trullion* and Jubal Droad of *Maske* act only to restore their homes and preserve them from change; they move only to keep from having to move. Jantiff of *Wyst* wants only to paint and travel a bit to enrich his visual store of experience. All discover, or know from the beginning, that going There, wherever There may be, is pointless.

Glinnes is the spokesman for the new set of values. Comfortably settled in a society where the favorite activity is gazing at the nighttime stars and telling stories about them, Glinnes is approached by a Fanscher, a member of the new movement for progress, who proposes to Glinnes that he join them in their plans to found a "college of dynamic formulations," an "academy of achievement" (*T*, 123). Glinnes replies,

> And...give up starwatching? By no means. I don't care whether I achieve anything or not. As for your college, if you laid it down on the meadow you'd spoil my view. Look at the light on the water yonder; look at the color of the trees! Suddenly it seems as if your talk of "achievement" and "meaning" is sheer vanity—the pompous talk of small boys (*T*, 124).

Vance means this—the light on the water *is* worth a lifetime's appreciative contemplation, and achievement spoils the view.

But long before Glinnes, the early heroes are learning that linear living, living with one's heart in the plot, is ultimately dissatisfying. Even when the plot doesn't abort, and we reach our goal by fair and sound plotting, the achievement cloys, and the pay-off tastes of dust, boredom, and death.

This pattern shows most clearly in the Demon Prince series, because the series contains Vance's very best plotting, and is centered around his most "forward-footed" hero, Kirth Gersen. When Gersen was a child, he witnessed the Mount Pleasant Massacre, in which five galactic villains joined to pillage and enslave Gersen's entire village, leaving only him and his grandfather alive. Gersen devotes his life to killing the five, having been drilled by his grandfather from childhood to age thirty in preparation. His grandfather trains him to obsession: "I guarantee you ample satisfaction," he says, "for I will teach you to crave the blood of these men more than the flesh of woman" (*StK*, 27)—or anything else. Gersen succeeds in killing one villain per novel, but grandfather's promise is not fulfilled: though Gersen sacrifices home, peace, love, friendship, everything in exchange for the big Prize of retribution, Vance makes sure that each triumph involves the destruction of something precious, and Gersen is left regretting his victory as much as exalting in it. His sense of regret and ambivalence grows with each supposed triumph.

In *The Star King*, the first of the novels, Gersen traps Malagate the Woe by offering him an irresistible prize: a virgin, paradisial planet unknown to sentient races, a place so beautiful that to gaze on it brings a pleasure close to pain. Malagate reveals himself and is killed, but in the process the planet is despoiled, and Gersen ends more sensitive of his violation of place than to his victory over Malagate.

In the second volume, *The Killing Machine*, Vance refines his theme of the linear hero who despoils single-mindedly. Gersen pursues Kokkor Hekkus, the Killing Machine, to his home planet of

Thamber, a semi-mythical fairy world of golden-haired knights, dragons, and black castles of evil. Thamber has been forgotten by the rest of the Galaxy, and there we discover that Hekkus has carefully bred the culture to be a paradise of self-indulgence, a Fantasy Island in which he plays all the fun parts. Using his hormagaunt power to change faces, he is simultaneously Hekkus, the dark knight of the dreaded Brown Bersaglars, and Sion Trumble, the golden prince of the forces of good, who strives to defeat Hekkus. Thamber, by Hekkus's careful orchestration, is acting out an endless cycle of high emotionalism, with Hekkus feeding on all the emotions. Hekkus even plans to abduct Sion Trumble's betrothed, and so rape his own bride. Into this fantasy kingdom enters Gersen, who exposes Hekkus, kills him, and leaves with the princess. The world, stripped of its hero, its devil, and its maiden *anima*, now emotionally bankrupt, drearily begins to reestablish contact with the mundane galaxy.

In the third volume, *The Palace of Love*, not only is the victory a despoilation, but we discover that the villain is a victim, more deserving of our sympathy than our hatred. Gersen pursues the sybaritic voluptuary Viole Falusche to Falusche's pleasure dome, the Palace of Love, where Falusche invites guests to enter into his ongoing experiments into the varieties and limits of pleasure. When Gersen kills Falusche, the Palace is disbanded, and the inhabitants, like the inhabitants of Thamber and the plant creatures of the planet in *Star King*, are evicted from their innocent, emotionally rich womb and sent into the chill of real life, their dreams pitilessly uprooted. Gersen oversees the dismantling of the Palace, like a government flunky resettling farmers thrown off their lands by freeway construction projects. But in the meantime, we've discovered that Falusche's secret is more pathetic than horrific: Falusche was an ugly, antisocial teenager jilted by a flirtatious high school jade named Jheral. Ever since, in his Palace labs, Falusche has been cloning Jheral's cells, trying to raise a Jheral to be indoctrinated into loving him. Each new Jheral takes an instinctive dislike to Falusche, and the round of rejection and supplication continues. Thus, Falusche is attempting to have his love reciprocated and undo an old wrong done to him by someone really worse than he, and Gersen's triumph over him seems almost misguided.

In the fourth volume, *The Face*, Gersen realizes that he and his enemy are on the same side. Gersen pursues the egomaniacal, ugly prankster, Lens Larque. Larque is working some monstrous scheme, and when Gersen kills him he figures out what it is. Larque is Darsh, a member of a coarse and filthy race. Once he had tried to buy a house in the exclusive neighborhood of the snooty Methlens. The Methlen next door forbade the sale, saying that he didn't want to see Larque's ugly Darsh face gazing over his fence every night. Larque in retaliation bought mining rights to Shanitra, the moon in the sky over the Methlens, and seeded it with explosives that would carve his own hideous face in it. Gersen kills Larque before the plunger can be thrown, but by this time he has come to share Larque's hatred for the Methlens— largely because Larque's would-be neighbor has a daughter who loves Gersen, but has spurned him because of class differences. Vance records Gersen's conversion:

> Lens Larque had labored long to achieve his most sardonic trick. Should such toil and expense be wasted, especially since Gersen shared all of Lens Larque's motivations? "No," said Gersen. "Of course not" (*F*, 224).

In a splendid revolt against his own career, Gersen joins forces with the dead Larque and pushes the plunger. He then phones his lover's father and says, "Go out into your back garden; there's a great Darsh face hanging over the garden wall," and hangs up.

The fifth and last volume, *The Book of Dreams*, does not continue Gersen's progress toward enlightenment. He seems disappointingly comfortable with his heroic role, and because of this the novel seems unsatisfying as a conclusion to the series. Gersen does, however, end his quest with a sense of emotional emptiness and loss: in the final paragraph, he says he feels "deflated" and "deserted by [his] enemies." And the plot does peak to a magnificently bathetic anti-climax: Gersen pursues Howard Alan Treesong from planet to planet, only to be locked in a cellar at the last moment by a sweet old couple whose aid he enlists to trap Treesong; they have their own scores to settle, and they dispatch the arch-villain with consummate ease and efficiency, while our superhero futilely chases after them in a handcar. Treesong, galactic emperor of crime, who has foiled the best-laid plans of Gersen, master thief-taker, is neatly trapped, trussed, and punished by Ma and Pa Kettle. Both hero and villain end their careers in a cloud of ignominy.

Over and over again through Vance's career, Vance's linear men get to their chosen goals only to find something fundamentally wrong with their quests. Typically, Vance's successful heroes are left staring into a void of uncertainty and idleness; instead of dwelling on their triumphs, they are left sitting in timid contemplation of their new, dearly-won aimlessness. In *The Dying Earth*, Vance's first novel, Guyal of Sfere seeks the Museum of Man to find the answers to the fundamental questions of life, slaying demons in his path, resisting temptations, winning his maiden, gaining access to all knowledge—the novel ends with him saying to his lover, "What shall we do..." The theme is repeated often: at the end of *Marune*, when the protagonist Efraim has won his woman and his estate and social preeminence, he again asks his lover Maerio, "So then—what shall we do?" This time the obvious answer is written out for us. Maerio answers, "I don't know," and the novel concludes with Efraim's response: "I don't know either." At the end of *The Dragon Masters* we see Joaz Banbeck, who has accomplished all he can think to strive for, wistfully tossing little pieces of rubble onto big piles of rubble—the products of his battles—the novel's last line is his,

"Where it all ends, no one knows less than I." And Vance's linear men often triumph only to discover that victory returns them to their starting places. Cugel the Clever is left at the end of *The Eyes of the Overworld* sitting on the exact stretch of beach from which he began his journey; and Etzwane of the Durdane series labors for three volumes, overthrows governments and forms new ones, wages wars, is captured by aliens and leads a revolution against them, to be left sitting in his old familiar native inn, having accomplished nothing, with his old boss, the bandleader, asking him if he wants back his old job in the band.

The problem with questing is summed up in one of Vance's archetypal characters, the pilgrim. For Vance, a pilgrim is a fool who pursues a will-of-the-wisp to give himself something to do. He fabricates a ludicrous goal for himself and devotes himself to it utterly, becoming, therefore, utterly blind to the here and now and the victim of any con artist. Pilgrims can only hope to quest forever, because reaching the Grail only opens the eyes to the hollowness of what one has spent a lifetime seeking.

This truth shows repeatedly in Vance's heroes' relationships with women. In Vance's world, women are like fanes or grails —prizes, objects to seek to possess. All Vance's heroes pursue women, and the pursuit almost always ends in one of two dissatisfying ways: either the hero simply wanders away from the chase, too busy to muster interest in it; or he wins his love, and finds that what was exciting in pursuit is pallid and lifeless in possession. This metaphor of the hollow prize is allegorized in *Emphyrio*, where the craftsmen of Amboy slave all their lives in service to, and in vain hopes of joining, the idolized Lords, who live lives of assumed, lavish self-indulgence in Eyries soaring high above the city. Ghyl Tarvoke questions this unjust distribution of labor, and ultimately discovers the culture's terrible secret: the Lords are *literally* hollow—puppets made by the puppetmasters of Damar to bleed the craftsmen of Amboy. The Eyries are husks, like movie sets.

Vance's linear heroes experience life generally as they experience women: satisfying consummation always eludes them. Sometimes, for instance, the hero finds that he has pursued the villain through the novel, only to find him and the entire dramatic situation solved by someone else. In *Maske*, Jubal closes in on the villainous Ramus Ymph, but before he can reach him, Ymph violates the customs of the Wael, a society of tree worshipers, and they turn him into a tree. Jubal, finding that the climax of the plot has taken place without him, takes Ymph back to the capitol and plants him in a memorial park.

Sometimes the hero finds that coincidence renders his entire quest irrelevant. In *Showboat World*, Apollon Zamp faces a dire problem: his showboat has been invited to voyage to the court of King Waldemar at Mornune to compete in the Grand Festival of the greatest showboats on the planet. But Zamp's splendid boat and crew are sabotaged by a spiteful competitor, and he must compete with a rag-tag crew and a boat financed by Gassoon, a dotty antiquarian who insists that all performances be of *Macbeth*. To add spice to the competition, all losing crews will be tortured. How can Zamp keep Gasson satisfied, and still restage *Macbeth* to outshine the most splendiferous spectacles of the other showboats? For the bulk of the novel, Zamp practices for the competition by playing *Macbeth* in various hilarious forms modified to tickle the local mores and eccentricities of the population centers along the shore of their river route to Mornune, usually with disastrous results. Zamp's fate looks dire, but we have seen how clever and resourceful he can be; and our appetites are whetted for whatever devious solution he can find at Mornune. None is forthcoming; the long awaited competition is cancelled when Zamp's mysterious female passenger reveals herself to be the rightful ruler of Mornune and deposes King Waldemar. The novel's other basic mystery (who is Lady Blanche-Astor?) has rendered moot the first (how will Zamp win the competition?). Yet another mystery renders mystery number two moot. Gassoon, who collects artifacts of antiquity, appears quite by chance at court in one of his possessions, a tabard which turns out to be the lost Holy Tabard, making him rightful ruler of Mornune and automatically deposing Blanche-Astor. Each resolution is more contrived and dramatically unmotivated than the one before. This Gilbert-and-Sullivan farce is put to an end when Gassoon, heir to Mornune, finds the court and the lady enervated and suffocating; and returns with Zamp to the real life, the river journey, free of the absurdities of places to go, contests to win, and ladies to woo.

The epic of Vancean anti-climax is the Durdane series, in which Vance writes three complex volumes to document the folly of linear living. The plot, by volumes: in *The Anome*, Gastel Etzwane sees his prostitute mother sent to the tannery unfairly, and sets out to find the Anome, the Faceless Man who—solitary, omnipotent, and omniscient—rules all of Durdane. Etzwane seeks to convince the Anome of the injustice done to his mother, and to get him to free her. Simultaneously he practices music, in imitation of his father, the legendary itinerant musician Dystar (whom he has never seen), and he dreams of one day meeting him. The borders of Durdane are being attacked by the Rogushkoi, savage and fecund man-like creatures, origin unknown, whose only aim in life seems to be destroying human males and capturing females for breeding. Before Etzwane can reach the capital city, his mother is killed in a Rogushkoi raid; but by then he has met Ifness, a man of urbane competence and unspecified motives, who interests him in the Rogushkoi. Together they go to the capital to ask the Anome why action against the Rogushkoi has not been forthcoming. The Anome is an awesome mystery—no one has ever known for sure that one even exists, but he decapitates all who err in Durdane, by some secret means. Ifness and Etzwane capture him with ease and find him to be one Sajarano, a second-rate nobleman of no pretension or force of character, who promises to do something about the Rogushkoi. Ifness reveals himself to be a representative of Earth's Historical Institute, who is finally recalled to Earth in disgrace for tampering with Durdane's culture.

In *The Brave Free Men*, the second book in the series, Etzwane realizes that Sajarano is dragging his feet, so he locks him in his room and assumes the post of Anome. He organizes a new government by ordering the docile civil service to create one, and forges a militia to fight the Rogushkoi. There seems to be a traitor in the new government who is slipping tactics to the Rogushkoi, and all evidence points to one Aun Sharah, but apparently he's innocent, and the matter is soon forgotten.

Meanwhile, Etzwane hears that his father is performing at a nearby tavern, and he goes to fulfill the lifelong dream of meeting him. They meet, and chat of insignificances. Etzwane chooses not to reveal to Dystar the bond between them, sensing that Dystar wouldn't care. Vance summarizes:

> Etzwane began to feel uncomfortable. A hundred times he had envisioned the meeting...,always in dramatic terms. Now they sat at the same table and the occasion was suffocated in dullness (*BFM*, 106).

Dystar never learns that Etzwane is his son.

The Rogushkoi apparently come from Palesedra, since the Palesedrans, reclusive and inscrutable neighbors, are known to experiment with genetic engineering. So Etzwane's militia drives the Rogushkoi toward Palesedra; however, the Rogushkoi escape in a spaceship, thus proving that they are off-world creations. Ifness, who has apparently been reinstated by the Historical Institute, has been studying Rogushkoi bodies in Palesedran labs, and reappears to explain all to a baffled Etzwane: the Rogushkoi, Sarajano, and others have been possessed by Asutra, alien parasites who occupy other creatures' innards and control them to as-yet-unknown ends.

Let's pause here at the end of volume two and count how many ways this plot has already failed to fulfill its dramatic promise: 1) Etzwane sets out to save his mother, but she is killed before he can take steps to save her; 2) Ifness is recalled in shame to Earth, and reappears without explanation when he is needed; 3) Etzwane dreams of meeting Dystar and claiming his father, but finds him entirely unable to support Etzwane's fantasy of him; 4) the dread Anome, invisible dispenser of justice to a planet's suppliant billions, is a mouse Etzwane sends to his room, and who is replaced by our self-appointed hero; 5) much of volume two is devoted to smoking out the traitor Aun Sharah, who actually isn't one, and who is soon forgotten; 6) the Palesedrans happen to make creatures much like the Rogushkoi, but that turns out to be a coincidence; 7) Etzwane overthrows one regime and appoints himself the head of a new one, simply by telling everyone that the Anome told him to; 8) Etzwane's war against the Rogushkoi leaves him baffled and without direction, and Ifness, the Fully-Informed Stranger, discourses at the end of the volume on all the information the plot has failed to discover.

But all this is only warm-up for volume three, *The Asutra*.

Etzwane and Ifness enter slaving territory to examine some Rogushkoi remains, and discover that the region's most notorious slaver is Asutra-controlled and is shipping great numbers of slaves off-world at the Asutra's command. Etzwane talks an unenthusiastic Ifness into calling for a warship from Earth to intervene, while Etzwane secrets himself aboard the slaver's depot ship hoping that Ifness's ship will arrive before the Asutra come to collect the hundreds of slaves gathered aboard. Ifness's help never arrives, and Etzwane is helplessly led to Kahei, the world of the Ka, where he and the other humans are drilled to fight in the Ka's militia. They are sent out to fight, but Etzwane turns the militia to revolt, returns to camp and captures it, then seizes an incoming spaceship and forces its crew to fly them home to Durdane. He returns to his old inn, where he finds Ifness, who impersonally and brutally shatters all of his heroic illusions.

At first Ifness doesn't even recall Etzwane's heroic attempt to rescue the slaves; when asked if he remembers the circumstances of their parting, he replies languidly, "I believe that you departed in pursuit of a barbarian maiden, or some such thing" (*As*, 197). Did he send to Earth for reinforcements, as he promised? He "mentioned the matter" to his superiors, but "nothing came of it" (*As*, 198).

While Etzwane was off playing hero, Ifness was getting results: continuing his studies in the lab, he now knows everything about the Asutra and the Ka, and he explains all—the psychology and history of the Asutra, the causes of their war with the Ka, the reasons for the Rogushkoi and the taking of human slaves, and on and on, pages of explication answering all the questions the plot has failed to reveal.

Finally, Ifness' history bursts Etzwane's last bubble. Ifness, armed with his complete understanding of the Asutra, requisitioned an Earth ship, flew to Kahei, and in cool administrative fashion settled the war; he also sent a ship to return the human slaves to their homeland. Thus Etzwane heroically captured a camp already captured by Ifness, and commandeered a ship sent to rescue him. To complete the humiliation, he was rescued impersonally, by a colleague who had forgotten Etzwane's involvement in the matter. Etzwane's own plot has been settled behind his back by Ifness's blase, sedentary competence, while Etzwane was off swashbuckling. He is fully humbled:

> Ifness [says], "You seem troubled; has my account distressed you in any way?"
> "Not at all," [says] Etzwane. "As you say, truth destroys many illusions."
> "As you can apprehend, I was preoccupied with large causes....What were your own actions subsequent to our parting?"
> "They were of no great consequence," [says] Etzwane. "After some small inconveniences, I returned to Shillinsk..." (*As*, 202).

Etzwane asks if he may join Ifness, and thus share Ifness's ability to be at the center of plots; Ifness refuses and leaves forever, leaving Etzwane stripped of illusion or direction, sitting bleakly in his tavern. Three volumes of grandiose quest have brought him to where he began, and the trilogy ends with a final, cruelly gentle disappointment: "He looked toward the door, though he knew that Ifness had gone."

The lowest level of Etzwane's failure is beneath the surface. Etzwane is born abandoned by his father, and soon loses his mother; in basic psychological terms, his quest is a search for a father figure. He woos three candidates, and they all fail or reject him. Dystar, the father of imaginative genius, is jaded and indifferent; Sarajano, the father of paternal authority, turns out to be a mouse, and Etzwane deposes him; Ifness, the father of rational competence, disowns him.

Yet Etzwane's quest has not been without its consequences: thanks to his efforts and those of Ifness, the Great Song of the Ka, the ancient, venerated, monumental work of art, product of countless years of esthetic maturation, has been lost, and the age-old tradition of oral transmission of the sacred knowledge interrupted. Again the hero has trampled greatness in his haste to a barren end. Etzwane asks Ifness if the later can undo the damage; Ifness says he might try.

In the Demon Prince series, there is an organization called the Institute, a group of wise patriarchs who use their wisdom and power primarily to restrain progress. At one point, an Over-Centennial Fellow of the Institution (i.e., Hundredth-Degree Black Belt) explains why, in their view, getting There is inherently undesirable:

> We of the Institute receive an intensive historical inculcation; we know the men of the past, and we have projected dozens of possible future variations, which, without exception, are repulsive. Man, as he exists now, with all his faults and vices, a thousand gloriously irrational compromises between two thousand sterile absolutes—is optimal (*KM*, 38).

For Vance, a hero is a person making the swiftest possible progress toward his chosen, sterile absolute.

Vance has written a beautiful parable on man's habit of living linearly in "The Men Return." Earth has "[swum] into a pocket of noncausality" (*EFM*, 280). Vance explains the significance:

> Man had dominated Earth by virtue of a single assumption: that an effect could be traced to a cause, itself the effect of a previous cause. Manipulation of this basic law yielded rich results...Man congratulated himself on his generalized structure...He was unaware of his vulnerability. When the Earth entered the pocket, ...all the ordered tensions of cause-effect dis-

solved. [Logic] was useless; it had no purchase on reality. Those who survived were the few so "strongly charged with the old causal dynamic" that they could keep their body metabolism obedient to the old laws; but those who thrived were the Organisms, the "lords of the era, their discords so exactly equivalent to the vagaries of the land as to constitute a peculiar wild wisdom" (*EFM*, 280).

In this new world, the future doesn't necessarily follow the present. Acts may be finished before they are begun. Any direction is as likely as any other to take you to a specific destination. In short, the concept of plot is the fundamental insanity. Vance dramatizes life in such a world with his usual brilliance, but in the end the Earth departs the pocket of non-causality and the old laws are again in force. An Organism elegizes, "The freedom is gone; the tightness, the constrictions are back!" (*EFM*, 287). The Organisms are quickly destroyed by the consequences of their actions—one walks on water and is surprised to drown—but the remaining rationalists, Finn and Gisa, know exactly what to do; the story concludes with the following words:

> Finn pointed here and there around the fresh new land. "In that quarter, the new city...Over there the farms, the cattle."
> "We have none of these," protested Gisa.
> "No," said Finn. "Not now. But once more the sun rises and sets, once more rock has weight and air has none..." He stepped forward over the fallen Organism. "Let us make plans."

Finn immediately sets off in a direction; now that "forward" has meaning again, he naturally goes that way—callously stepping over carcasses and other trivial things in his haste. Finn is a parody of Vance's linear men, who can only survive in progress toward something; and the story's greatness lies partly in its ability to capture the tedious dullness of Finn's "let's get to work on that city *now!*" mentality, and the devil-may-care high spirits of the Organisms' alternative. We mourn the loss of the non-causal world—where absurdity and madness make as much sense as anything else and every act has magical, unforeseeable consequences—and when it passes, we too feel the tightness, the constriction.

The drive to comprehend and thus dominate the universe, to determine Outcome, the force behind scientific inquiry and the fundamental myth of science fiction—"If I know enough, I can control *everything*"—is finally repudiated by Vance in almost every one of his works. The alternatives to linear living, the ancient, static, timeless things of real value, are evident throughout his work; they are the things we remember from his story long after the efforts at plotting are forgiven and forgotten: a complex and eccentric culture, a pungent alien odor, a meal of nauseating native dishes, the bittersweet beauty of a tranquil voyage under skies of mauve and scarlet—the sensual intensity of the moment, and the priceless heritage of the past. Vance's early heroes rush *through* these things on the way to somewhere, ignoring or destroying them; the late novels ask us to sit and steep in them, breathing in the rich cultural resonances. The Institute is right: all futures are repulsive. But look at the light on the water yonder; look at the color of the trees!

V
AFTERWORD: NEW DIRECTIONS

I think I can promise you a total palliation.

Since the first draft of this study was completed in 1981, Vance has published several major new books, including *Cugel's Saga* (1983), *Lyonesse* (1983), *Rhialto the Marvellous* (1984), and *The Green Pearl* (1985). What do these new titles suggest about Vance's art and where it might be heading?

Vance's career falls into three fairly distinct periods. In the first, from 1945 to the middle Fifties, Vance imitated Establishment SF of the time, the "Golden Age" which was dominated by the values of *Astounding*'s John W. Campbell. The emphasis here was on the clever idea or provocative hypothesis as the story's center, spiced with hard technological science. The topics were those of traditional SF: psionics, immortality, and the values those of progressive, jingoistic, freedom-loving Americans.

The second period began with a bang in 1957-58, when Vance published five works that announced his departure from the "mainstream" of science fiction and signalled his new orientation: *Big Planet*, "The Miracle Workers," "The Men Return," *The Languages of Pao*, and "Coup de Grace." These works include the dominant features of his work for the next seventeen years: the emphasis on the alien esmeric; the fascination with cultural relativism; the arbitrariness of cultural conventions, and their power to ossify and enslave societies; his vision of cultural history as a pendulum swinging back and forth between sterile, antithetical absolutes; and his definition of social health as a melting-pot intermix of those extremes. Stories become less interested in technological hardware and more interested in exotic persons and places. Jingoism becomes the ultimate unwisdom, and Vance's heroes become less confident and arrogant as a result.

The third period began in 1973, with the publication of *The Anome* and *Trullion*, the initial volumes in two series of books in which the quest is found to be utterly barren. Plots go nowhere, heroes are abandoned in befuddlement, and Vance's novels become devoted to locales and their esmeric alone. The value system is now often boldly anti-intellectual—progress is an illusion, and real happiness can only be found in stasis.

Such a career suggests no obvious next place to go, and there are signs that Vance isn't having an easy time finding a new direction. Of the three recent titles, two are extensions of something that has worked well in the past. *Rhialto* contains three new stories concerning the activities of the magicians of the Dying Earth; and *Cugel* is a sequel to *The Eyes of the Overworld*, in which Cugel is once again transported to the sticks by his nemesis Iucounu the Laughing Magician, and forced to work his way home through a series of road adventures. Some of the new work is very good—parts of *Cugel* are among the funniest, cleverest in Vance's rogue literature—but it represents no new vision.

Lyonesse, on the other hand, is a clear and conscious attempt to find a new direction, or at least to find a new audience. It differs from Vance's earlier work in a number of ways, most of them attempts to write a less idiosyncratic, more easily read book, and thereby reach a larger, more traditional audience. It's set in the romantic past, not in the future or on an alien world: it takes place in the Elder Isles, a group of long-since-vanished islands just off the west coast of Europe, two generations before the mythic Arthur's reign in Britain. The world is largely that of classical and medieval fantasy—fairies, knights, magicians in dark castles—not a world of unique Vancean invention; and the style, while unmistakably Vance, is less Byzantine and closer to the medieval fantasy norm. The plot is drawn from classical European mythology—babies switched in cradles by fairies, solitary princesses who dwell in secret gardens, and the like. The central event is borrowed whole-cloth from Homer's *Odyssey*: the hero, Aillas, is dumped overboard during a passage at sea, and is washed ashore to be brought back from the dead and loved by the Princess Suldrun. And the central theme—two hostile noble houses united, despite the parents' attempts to prevent it, by the tragic love of their offspring—is equally traditional.

In some ways the book has obviously been influenced by current marketing trends. The book is deliberately long (436 p.), and is merely the first volume of a trilogy. It treats the interwoven lives of several great families, follows several plot lines at once, and has a strong sense of dynasty. It has explanatory apparatus in appendices, in the manner of Tolkien or Herbert, despite the fact that this is a direct violation of one of Vance's virtues: that the rules of the alien world *emerge* from our experience living in it, not by direct narrative exposition. And there is a gay couple, which may or may not be a bow to trendiness.

Despite all this, the book remains wholly Vancean: full of strange beauty, picaresque adventure, astounding cruelty and violence, sexual degradation of women, sardonic philosophy, ingeniously crafted escapes, and rococo language. People, when they're about to kill their enemies horribly, still say things like, "I think I can promise you total palliation" (*L*, 364). Whether *Lyonesse* will prove a successful experiment, whether Vance has finally found a way to present his particular virtues in ways more accessible to conventional palates, remains to be seen. Only this is certain: whatever Jack Vance publishes in the future, in long or short form, will continue to bear his own unique stamp as an author, that sense of exotic originality which makes most other writers in a very creative field seem tame by comparison.

VI
AN INTERVIEW WITH JACK VANCE

The bad stuff I forget.

In January of 1985 I telephoned Jack Vance and asked him if he would be willing to talk with me about his life and his work. He groaned and sighed, and reiterated his famous hatred of discussing either of those topics. I asked why, and he said interviewers always wanted him to say something profound, which he was unable to do; or something embarrassing about other SF writers, which he was unwilling to do. I promised to be kind. "I don't know what to say," he concluded unenthusiastically. I showed up at his home in the Oakland hills with tape recorder in hand and heart in mouth. I was welcomed as a friend and valued guest, and Vance spoke playfully, volubly, and astutely until I ran out of tape. Here are some excerpts from our conversation.

VANCE: I'll set the ball rolling. "Well, Vance, what the hell are you doing with yourself?" That's a good question, Jack. I just finished the second volume in the Lyonesse Cycle, and so...I'm not doing anything. I've got a contract for three new books, and the third book in the Lyonesse set, and I'm just sitting back stupified by the magnitude of this task.

RAWLINS: How's business? You're very busy. Are you doing well?

VANCE: Well, it's relative. Compared to Isaac Asimov, I'm striving for every last crust of bread. Compared to some Patagonian aborigine, I'm doing fine.

RAWLINS: When I first met you, it seemed like nobody had heard of you then except your immediate family, and now you've won a tidy reputation and found publishers who take you seriously and want you to write for them. Fifteen years ago I asked you why you didn't write the last two Demon Princes books, and you said, "I'd be glad to write them if anybody would pay me for them." That's no longer a problem.

VANCE: I don't know. I guess so. I suppose the reputation is growing a little bit, but I don't think there's any great mushroom cloud...I still don't have the mass public that even Ray Bradbury has.

RAWLINS: You must be the most honored "Little Name" in SF: two

Hugos, one Nebula, one Jupiter, and an Edgar for your mystery fiction.

VANCE: This last year they threw a...what the hell's the name of that thing?—H.P. Lovecraft?—at me supposedly for "lifetime achievement." Apparently their system for giving them out was to select the guy who looked to be on his last legs, and give one to him so he could have it as his eyes faded, so it's kind of the kiss of death.

RAWLINS: *Lyonesse* appears to be a somewhat more conventional, more easily categorizable and marketable book than your earlier work.

VANCE: That was done purposely. I thought I'd try to catch some lending library ladies. And the book's sold pretty well. But my audience is still very specialized: highly intelligent young men.

RAWLINS: When I started it I was hesitant, because it looked more like things a lot of other people were doing; but I was happy to see that it's still very much in harmony with what you've done before.

VANCE: You're accurate on both counts. I didn't compromise on the intellectual level, but I dealt with things I thought the general public might be more at ease with.

RAWLINS: How are the publishers treating you these days? I know many of your early titles aren't of your choosing. Do your books come out the way you want them to now?

VANCE: Now they do!

RAWLINS: I know *Big Planet* went through some radical cuts.

VANCE: I didn't mind the cuts so much, but they changed the names without asking me, which irked me no end. But then I didn't have any clout; I was happy to get five hundred bucks for a book.

RAWLINS: What about some of your other titles?

VANCE: One very early book called *Bird Island* was renamed by the publisher *Isle of Peril*, which was foolish, because there wasn't any peril in it. *To Live Forever* wasn't my title—I don't like that title. *Showboat World* I called *The Magnificent Showboats of the Lower Vissel River: Cusp 23, Big Planet*; they didn't like that, and called it *Showboat World*, which I think is a rotten title. *Cugel's Saga* isn't my title—I hate it. *The Effectuator* was changed to *The Galactic Effectuator*.

I don't like the title *Space Opera*, but since I was commissioned to write a novel with that title I couldn't complain.

RAWLINS: You mean you're sometimes commissioned to write a book to fit a title?

VANCE: Sure. I wrote "The Augmented Agent" to fit a cover. I went to a party, and a publisher of *Planet Stories* said she had gotten some artist's paintings cheap. I got two. One showed some giant moths attacking a person, so I wrote around that the story called "Ecological Onslaught," which is a rotten title. The other one showed a row of missiles in silos in the water along a coast. I wrote "Augmented Agent" for that one.
  I did another story around a cover, showing a bunch of sails in space. Turned out to be one of the best short stories I ever wrote—"Sail 25."

RAWLINS: Which was also originally called something odd: "Gateway to Strangeness."

VANCE: That was for another reason. The editor had to set up the magazine cover before he knew what the story was going to be called, so he just decided that whatever the story was about it would be called "Gateway to Strangeness."

RAWLINS: Anyone interested in turning one of your stories into a movie?

VANCE: Once, in the Fifties—from one of the Magnus Ridolph stories ("Hard Luck Diggings")—worst story I ever wrote. Some producer saw it, and I guess he liked the idea of intelligent trees. It didn't come to anything.
  At that time I had set out to become a million-word-a-year man. So I hid out in a relative's house over a weekend and wrote the first two Magnus Ridolph stories—first drafts. I don't think I've ever reread them.

RAWLINS: How do you write now? Do you write slowly? Do you rewrite?

VANCE: I've got my writing down, and I'm pretty disciplined, so I don't have to do a lot of rewriting. I like to write about two or three thousand words a day, and I like to write straight through the whole first draft of the book without rewriting, then go back and do the whole second draft at once. But I find that in the morning I glance at the stuff of the day before, see something needing to be changed, and get caught up—pretty soon I'm completely rewriting the day's work.
  The word processor has really increased my volume. I used to write longhand, my wife would type it out, I'd go through it again, and she'd type it out again. Damn, she did a lot of work. But that was the only way to do it, because I couldn't type—it's too rigid.

RAWLINS: You have a famous reputation as a recluse. Are you?

VANCE: I like having the reputation. It adds a kind of glamor.

RAWLINS: Asimov's introductions to your two stories in *The Hugo Winners*—*Last Castle* and *The Dragon Masters*—are both about what a mystery man you are. The first says in effect, "SF is one big happy family. We all go to conventions and goof around together —except Vance." The second says, in effect, that you're impossible to locate, but he managed to find someone who said he knew you, from whom he wrested a stray biographical fact or two. This is the Vancean myth, yet your home phone is listed in the phone book, you answer your own phone, and as far as I know you've welcomed anyone who has come here in friendship.

VANCE: Not everyone. I just don't enjoy going to conventions and goofing around. And I generally don't answer letters from anybody.

RAWLINS: Asking a writer about the craft is always anticlimactic. The first time I met you I asked you everyone's favorite Jack Vance question—"Where did you learn your wonderful vocabulary?" —and you said, "I use the thesaurus a lot." But I teach people how to write, so I'm interested in how people learn to do it. How did you learn?

VANCE: First of all, I think your occupation is like tits on a bull. No one can teach anybody how to write. People go to writing classes because they want to write and they grab at any straw. The best I think you can do is teach people punctuation, spelling...and conceivably put the idea of rhythm in their heads. Aside from that, what can you teach them?

I think the best way to teach someone to be a writer is to force them to read twenty books I would set out for them: *Don Quixote*, *Wind in the Willows*, works of P. G. Wodehouse, the Oz books, *The London Times Historical Atlas* (my favorite book—I don't know of anything that's more clutching for the imagination), *Watership Down*—there must be others on that list.

Watership Down might be the last book I read, actually. It's a great work of art; it creates a unique mood. I think the author got something there he wasn't even expecting to get. He just got swept away...and he tried to do other books and just fell flat on his face.

RAWLINS: That book isn't written; it just happens.

VANCE: Exactly right. I won't ever read it again.

RAWLINS: Elsewhere you've described yourself in your youth as standing impatiently by the mailbox eagerly awaiting the latest issue of *Weird Tales*. Is that an accurate portrait?

VANCE: Yes. We lived in the country, and the mailbox was about a quarter of a mile from the house. I knew about the day it was supposed to arrive...

RAWLINS: What made you decide to become a writer? Did you feel like you had something to say?

VANCE: No, no, no, no. I wanted freedom, and the only way I could think of to be free was to be a writer. I started in university as a mining engineer, changed to a physics major, but I just couldn't see myself in it—both those occupations seemed so claustrophobic—so I changed to English, History, journalism. And about that time I figured I'd better take this career thing seriously. In my sophomore English class I had to do a paper every week, so I decided to write a story, turn it in, and try to sell it. When the batch of stories was returned, the instructor said to the class, "This week, we run the gamut. On the one hand, we have, written by Mr. Smith, this beautiful, pungent story of a prize fight, in which you can smell the rosin and feel every blow. On the other hand, written by a person who shall be nameless, we have this piece of so-called science fiction."

RAWLINS: So that's when you knew... Which are your favorites among your works?

VANCE: *Palace of Love*—because of the mad poet, Navarth. And I like the last two [Demon Prince] books: *The Face* and *Book of Dreams*. Of course you know the symbol in Treesong's book got printed upside down in the DAW edition. It was supposed to look like a symbolic representation of pure spirit dynamically driving through space; it ended up looking like a beached whale.

RAWLINS: Who do you read these days?

VANCE: I never read anything in SF. I stopped reading that long, long, long ago. Haven't read anything for forty years.

RAWLINS: What about other things?

VANCE: I used to read murder mysteries—go on a binge every two or three years.

RAWLINS: Do you feel that the turn away from hard SF in the last ten years and toward fantasy has resulted in a break for you?

VANCE: I don't pay much attention to trends. If you tell me there's been a turn to fantasy, I'll accept it, but I don't read the books myself.

RAWLINS: Among fantasy writers, your work is remarkably "hard"—logically sound, interested in problems of the head. You love to write about escapes from physical imprisonment, siege tactics, and battle strategies, for instance. Yet you're often connected with the world of Dungeons and Dragons and sword and sorcery, which is usually thought of as juvenile escapist emotionalism.

VANCE: I wouldn't even consider myself a fantasy writer; I totally reject that—dragons and such like. My fantasy stuff I can number on the fingers of one hand: *The Dying Earth*, which is very early, and the other Dying Earth books, and the Lyonesse books.

RAWLINS: Yet even in your "fantasy" books there's a great respect for the operation of the intellect—in *The Eyes of the Overworld*, there are episodes like Cugel's escape from the tower in the Mountains of Magnatz, a perfect little lesson in logistical problem-solving. And all your heroes can do that...

VANCE: Competence—they have competence. Have you read *Cugel's Saga*?

RAWLINS: Yes. I like very much the scene in the tavern where Cugel and Bunderwal are trying to con each other out of the job on the boat.

VANCE: Yes. I think of that and laugh sometimes. The problem with writing the Cugel stuff is that you can't allow it to become farce. Because it's supposed to be...fantasy, or—but yet...I don't like the word fantasy, come to think of it. I think of it as straightforward adventure within the premises I establish for that world. Except for a couple of books where I made the mistake of putting some ideology in there...

RAWLINS: I think fantasy always has the connotation of mindless wish-fulfillment: let's have a good scare, fall in love, cleave a few skulls with swords...
One of the things that makes your work remarkable is the way it changes point of view, mood, temperament so often. Your books refuse to be just one sort of thing. *Lyonesse* is a perfect example: it juxtaposes stirring heroism, truly disturbing violence and cruelty, slapstick, bitter dark comedy, satire, pastoral romance, logical problem-solving, swashbuckling adventure. So the reader is having to shift gears at a moment's notice—one page he's gasping with horror and the next roaring with laughter. For instance, in the middle of the long and otherwise unrelievedly grim portrait of Cosmir's court, there's that brief, poignant interchange between Suldrun and her ineffectual but loving tutor Maister James, so gentle and sweet it brings tears to your eyes. Then, of course, you make us pay for caring by killing James off in an especially unsatisfying way. Compare that to, say, Tolkien or Herbert, where the tone, the point of view, the way I read, are the same page after page through the whole book. Do you do this intentionally?

VANCE: Yes, I try to...how to express it?...change the key, so to speak.

RAWLINS: I suspect that makes the reader work a lot harder, makes you harder to read.

VANCE: I know I'm writing for people to read, but long ago I decided I wouldn't make concessions to the low end of the readership—that I'd be always writing to the high end of the readership, and the low end would have to look out for themselves. I wouldn't condescend...because that's no fun.
    I'll tell you the truth. I have a competitive streak in me, and I'm happy that my "reputation" as you call it is finally seeping out; and occasionally I'll get a little critical notice in the world of legitimate, "mainstream" fiction, and I get a little chuckle—someone's picking up the wavelength at last.

RAWLINS: Your work is predominantly written against a backdrop of melancholic loss and the failure of heroic or romantic expectation. Your heroes generally refuse to play the hero. Gersen, for instance, is self-confessedly dour and bland. Your heroines refuse to think of themselves as romantic objects, and often grouse through the books being attractive in spite of their best attempts to be obnoxious, frigid, and gloomy. Your plots tend to end with loud doubts by the quester as to whether the quest was wise in the first place. Most of your best work— *The Dying Earth*, *The Last Castle*, "The Miracle Workers," *The Dragon Masters*—is about the death by attrition, stagnation, or richly deserved revolution of ancient, moribund, yet abundantly rich cultures. Your worlds frequently sport vastly old, precious cultural artifacts—like the Song of the Ka—and the pursuit of the quest almost always results in those artifacts getting trampled in its path.

VANCE: I have a strong sense of loss. We just got back from Europe, where we visited Corsica for the first time. I was curious about the place. I envisioned it as being wild, primitive. I'd even heard somewhere that there were still brigands in the interior. I believed it—the home of the vendetta, you know. But Europe has discovered the group tour, and it's devouring all its capital of beauty and privacy in pursuit of the quick buck of mass tourism. And so everywhere in Corsica there were hotels and highrises. The locals don't like it, but can't stop it. It's very sad to see; the place is being ravished, devoured. It isn't the tourists' fault.

RAWLINS: In your books the trampling usually isn't malicious; these artifacts just get in the way.

VANCE: This has been going on forever. Genghis Khan sweeping through Asia, destroyed city after city, their priceless scrolls and miniatures; some witless Christians burnt the library at Alexandria; Spanish Christians burned all the Incan art.

RAWLINS: Your later work has a profound sense of the importance of home—family estates, especially.

VANCE: Oh, yes. I love my home—this house, or any one I'm living in at the moment. Even California...even Oakland, I feel affection for.

RAWLINS: Your family is Old Californian, isn't it?

VANCE: Quite old, yes, many generations. My grandfather came out from Michigan about 1875. My grandmother was born in San Francisco. That must have been in the Sixties. I've been trying to find out, but all the records were lost in the [San Francisco] Fire. The Fire stopped a couple of blocks away from my grandfather's house.

RAWLINS: The character of your heroes has changed a lot since your early days; in books like *The Five Gold Bands* the hero tears around accomplishing things right and left. Lately things seem to have slowed down.

VANCE: That's because I slowly came to realize that people don't act like Paddy Blackthorne [hero of *FGB*]. I don't want to write about Conan or Tarzan; I want to write about human beings, under the influence of some extraordinary motivation.

RAWLINS: One of the best features of Gersen [hero of the Demon Prince novels] is your notion, which is with him from the beginning, that if he's going to devote his life to accomplishing this great deed, he's going to have to give up an awful lot. We almost never acknowledge this about our heroes; we want our athletes to be obsessively dedicated, but we want them to lose none of their warmth, their humanity, their simplicity, their honor, their accessibility, their ties to spouse and family in so doing.

VANCE: That's right.

RAWLINS: In each of the Demon Prince books, something happens to taint the sweetness of Gersen's victory, and in *The Book of Dreams* he actually gets robbed of the pleasure of killing the villain; that sweet old couple steps in and steals his thunder.

VANCE: I did that because I just couldn't envision Gersen standing there face to face and pulling the trigger on someone as vital as [Howard Alan] Treesong. So I got someone else to do it. There's a nobility about Treesong; he's an elemental force of nature. You might kill him, but without gloating—like you'd kill a rattlesnake.

RAWLINS: Heinlein once said that when he writes a book he imagines someone standing in the store with two dollars in hand trying to choose between a six-pack and the book, and he concluded, "I try to be better than beer." I get the impression you think more highly of your work than that. Is that true?

VANCE: Yes, I think it's true.

RAWLINS: You mentioned that you like "Sail 25." So do I. The characterization of the instructor..."

VANCE: Henry Belt.

RAWLINS: ...is as deep and subtle as any in SF. Which suggests a problem: you're not supposed to be able to write like that. And that's typical of your work: it refuses to stay within other people's tidy categories. Interviewers keep asking you to name the writers who influence you, in a desperate attempt to figure out which pigeonhole you fit into. They always go away disappointed. You write hard, empiricist problem-solving SF like *The Blue World*. You write penetrating social satire the New Wave would have been proud to write. You write anthropological SF that stands up well to Le Guin's. You're a master stylist in the manner of Bradbury or Bester. You're knock-down funny like Retief. You have the mythic emotional grandeur of the high fantasists. You write taut, dashing dramatic adventure when it's time for it. You are one of the very few SF writers who takes joy in language play and language use, as a medium. You delight in setting for yourself staggeringly difficult writer's tasks, like describing alien musical performances or the imagist competition in "The New Prime." [JV: "Yeah, that's fun."] And all this really in addition to what you're renowned for: the creation of weird, eldritch, static worlds of suggested emotions without earthly names. You seem to be a classic example of a writer who's been hurt by the need to put writers and books in categories. I know lots of people who would love your work except they refuse to read anything with a sword or a spaceship in it.

VANCE: It really drives me up the wall to be thought of as a sword-and-sorcery writer. And space ships are just devices for getting from one environment to another.

RAWLINS: Do you share my sense that you ought to be a titan in the field? Do you have a high regard for your work?

VANCE: You're damn right I do.

RAWLINS: I notice you remember your own work very well.

VANCE: The bad stuff I forget!

VII
SELECTIVE SECONDARY BIBLIOGRAPHY

We cannot unlock the doors,
but we can batter them open.

I have not attempted to include here all the hundreds of reviews of Vance's work that have appeared in the SF magazines (most of them perfunctory), or the editor's prefaces to Vance's stories in anthologies. All reviews (eight of *Big Planet*, for instance) can be located through the volumes of H. W. Hall's *The Science Fiction Book Review Index* (available from Borgo Press).

Allen, Paul C. "Of Swords and Sorcery," *Fantasy Crossroads* #9 (August 1976).

Ash, Brian. "Jack Vance." In *Who's Who in Science Fiction.* New York: Taplinger, 1976.

Blish, James. Review of *Eight Fantasms and Magics. The Magazine of Fantasy and Science Fiction* (April 1970).

Boardman, John. "Durdane: Or Is It America?" *Amra* #61 (1974).

Chandler, A. Bertram. "An Appreciation of Jack Vance." *Science Fiction* (June 1982).

Close, Peter. "An Interview with Jack Vance." *Science Fiction Review* #6 (November 1977).

Cockrum, Kurt, Daniel Levak, and Tim Underwood. *Fantasms 2.1: A Bibliography of the Published Fiction of Jack Vance.* Unpublished. 1979, 1980. By far the most complete bibliography of Vance's work, including discussions of the differences between works as they appeared in magazines and as novels, and all translations of Vance's writings into other languages.

Cox, Arthur Jean. "The Boredom of Fantasy." *Riverside Quarterly* #1 (1964).

Dickinson, Mike. "Romance and Hardening Arteries: A Reappraisal of the SF of Jack Vance." *Vector* #95 (1979).

Dowling, Terry. "The Art of Xenography: Jack Vance's "General Culture' Novels." *Science Fiction* #1 (December 1978).

_____. "Kirth Gersen: the Other Demon Prince." *Science Fiction* (June 1982).

_____. "A Xenographical Postscript (Containing, Among Other Sundry Matters, Certain Unsolicited Revelations Concerning Mr. Ryl Shermatz and Baron Bodissey)." *Science Fiction* #2.

"The Dragon Masters." In *Survey of Science Fiction Literature*, edited by Frank N. Magill. Englewood Cliffs, NJ: Salem Press, 1979.

"The Dying Earth." In *Fantasy Literature: A Core Collection and Reference Guide*. ed. Marshall B. Tymn et al. New York: R. R. Bowker, 1979.

"The Dying Earth." In *Survey of Science Fiction Literature*, ed. Frank N. Magill. Englewood Cliffs, NJ: Salem Press, 1979.

Edwards, Malcolm J. "Jack Vance." In *The Science Fiction Encyclopedia*. Garden City, Doubleday, 1979.

_____. "Jack Vance, 1916-". In *Science Fiction Writers: Critical Studies of the Major Authors from the Early Nineteenth Century to the Present Day*. Ed. Everett F. Bleiler. New York: Scribner's, 1982.

_____. "A Study in Anomie." *The Many worlds of Jack Vance/Horns of Elfland* #2 (1978).

"The Eyes of the Overworld." In *Fantasy Literature: A Core Collection and Reference Guide*, ed. Marshall B. Tymn et al. New York: R. R. Bowker, 1979.

"The Languages of Pao." In *Survey of Science Fiction Literature*, ed. Frank N. Magill. Englewood Cliffs, NJ: Salem Press, 1979.

"The Last Castle." In *Survey of Science Fiction Literature*, ed. Frank N. Magill. Englewood Cliffs, NJ: Salem Press, 1979.

Levak, Daniel, and Tim Underwood. *Fantasms: A Bibliography of the Literature of Jack Vance*. San Francisco: Underwood-Miller, 1978.

Malzberg, Barry. "Introduction," in *The Best of Jack Vance*. New York: Pocket Books, 1976.

The Many Worlds of Jack Vance, edited by Robbert Offutt, Jr., Pinson, AL. A fanzine devoted to Vance's work.

McFerran, Dave. "The Magic of the Dying Earth." *Anduril* #6 (1976).

Rawlins, Jack. "Linear Man: Jack Vance and the Value of Plot in Science Fiction." *Extrapolation* 24 (Winter 1983).

Reginald, R. *Science Fiction and Fantasy Literature: a Checklist, 1700-1974 with Contemporary Science Fiction Authors II*, vol. 1, p. 526; vol. 2, p. 1109.

Robson, Alan. "Jack Vance—the Magic and the Mystery." *Science Fiction Forum* (Winter 1977).

Russ, Joanna. Review of *Emphyrio*. *The Magazine of Fantasy and Science Fiction* (January 1970).

Searles, Baird, et al. "Jack Vance." In *A Reader's Guide to Science Fiction*. New York: Avon Books, 1979.

Tuck, Donald. "Jack Vance." In *The Encyclopedia of Science Fiction and Fantasy*. Chicago: Advent, 1978.

Underwood, Tim. "A Talk with Jack Vance" (interview). *The Many Worlds of Jack Vance* #1 (Spring 1977).
_____, and Chuck Miller, eds. *Jack Vance*. New York: Taplinger, 1980. Eight critical essays on Vance, by Peter Close, Terry Dowling, Robert Silverberg and others, plus a bibliography of Vance's work, a critical bibliography, and a biography.

INDEX

Abbatram of Pamfile, 16
Aillas, 87
Akadie, Janno, 19
Alastor series, 71, 73
Alien (movie), 18
Alouan, 19, 39, 44
Aloysians, 25
Alusz Iphegenia, 12, 29
Amboy, 20, 29, 41, 43-44, 62
Ambrosians, 25
Anacho, Ankhe at Afram, 25-26, 33-34
Anderson, Poul, 11
Anome, The, 23, 71, 80-81, 86
Ao Hiddis, 13, 15
Arma-Geth, 31
Asimov, Isaac, 49, 75, 88, 91
Asutra, The, 81-83
"Augmented Agent, The," 90
"Avatar's Apprentice, The," 28, 50, 74
awaile, 15, 33
Banbeck, Joaz, 26, 56, 62, 67, 75, 78-79
Basics, 46, 56, 62, 67
Batman, 71
Battle of Rudyer Moor, 25, 37
Beit, Henry, 96
Bester, Alfred, 12, 57, 96
Big Planet, 10, 37, 45, 68-69, 86
Blackthorne, Paddy, 27, 29, 67, 95
Blanche-Astor, Damsel, 80
Blue World, The, 33-34, 39-41, 46, 67-68, 74, 96
Bodissey, Baron, 16-17, 56
Bonfils, 37
Bonze, The, 37
Book of Dreams, The, 12, 16, 21, 35-36, 43, 47-48, 78, 92, 95
Bradbury, Ray, 49, 88, 96
Brave Free Men, The, 71, 81
Byzantaurs, 13, 24
Calbyssians, 13, 41
Campbell, John W., 14, 27, 49, 75, 86
Caraz, 27, 43
Carnevalle, 33
Castle Hagedorn, 40, 42, 56
Cath, 13, 15, 33, 38, 40-41, 43, 62, 69
Chasch and Chaschmen, 12-13, 31, 62

Chilites, 24
City of the Chasch, 10, 20, 31, 33, 45, 56, 58, 62
Cizante, Blue Lord of Cath, 38
Connatic, The, 35, 71, 73
"Coup de Grace," 37, 86
Cox, Arthur Jean, 28, 61
Cugel, 10, 12, 24, 26, 30-31, 38-39, 63-64, 69, 79, 87, 93
Cugel's Saga, 86-87, 89
Darsch, 63, 77-78
Darth Vader, 21
Demie, The, 26
Demon Prince series, 10, 16, 36-37, 43, 47-48, 60, 67-68, 72, 76, 88, 92, 95
Dickens, Charles, 21
Dirdir and Dirdirmen, 12-13, 31, 37, 41, 50, 70
Dirdir, The, 31-32, 43, 50
Discriminators, 23
Disjerferact, 33
Dissane (D. Drosset), 73
Djan, 56
"Dodkin's Job," 39-41
Dragon Masters, The, 10, 25, 39, 45, 67, 75, 78-79, 91, 94
Droad, Jubal, 62, 73, 75, 79
Drosset, Vang, 73-74
Dune, 12, 24, 69
Dungeons and Dragons, 20, 92-93
Durdane series, 19, 22, 27, 30-32, 34, 39, 43, 68, 70-71, 79-83
Dying Earth, The, 10, 19, 47, 57, 75, 78, 87, 93-94
Dystar, 19, 26, 55, 80-83
Earth, 31, 46-47, 68-69, 80
"Ecological Onslaught," 90
Edelrod, 28-29, 46
Edgar Award, 11, 89
Efraim, Kaiark of Scharrode, 72, 78
Eight Fantasms and Magics, 60
Eiselbar, 41
Emblemen, 69-70
Eminence, The, 29, 50, 74
Empire Strikes Back (movie), 21, 23
Emphrio, 10, 20, 25-26, 33-34, 39-40, 43, 71, 75, 79
Erdenfreude, 47
Erjelbar, 33
esmeric, 18ff., 28-29, 45, 86
Etzwane, Gastel, 14-18, 23, 26-31, 47, 61, 63, 70-71, 79, 80-83
Eyes of the Overworld, 10, 12, 24, 37, 68-69, 79, 87, 93
Face, The, 25, 47, 77-78, 92
Falusche, Viole, 18, 32, 48, 77
fanscherade, 45, 73-74, 76
Farr, Aile, 46, 68
Fianella of the Thousand Candles, 37
Five Gold Bands, The, 27, 67, 74, 95
Floats, 44, 68

Funambulous Evangels, 14, 25
Fwai-chi, 14, 45, 72
Galactic Effectuator, The, 89
Gassoon, 38, 79-80
Gensifer, Lord, 74
Gerrold, David, 21, 23
Gersen, Kirth, 10-13, 17-18, 22, 26-30, 36, 46-48, 63-68, 72, 76-78, 94-95
Glay (G. Hulden), 73
Glinnes (G. Hulden), 20, 73-76
Glissam, Elvo, 19
Golickan Kodek, 31
Gray Prince, The, 19, 34, 39, 43-45, 47
Green Pearl, The, 86
Grogatch, Luke, 41
Guild of Assassins, 43
Guyal of Sfere, 19, 26, 59, 62, 75, 78
Hableyat, 26
"Hard Luck Diggings," 90
Hast, Sklar, 30, 46, 67-68
Heinlein, Robert A., 21, 24, 49, 62, 95
Hekkus, Kokkor, 12, 32, 35-36, 46, 58, 72, 76-77
Herbert, Frank, 11-12, 23, 55, 69, 87, 93
Historical Institute, 27, 70-71, 80-81
Holmes, Sherlock, 66
Houses of Iszm, The, 37, 46, 68
Hugo Award, 10, 89
hussade, 19, 22, 74
Ifness, 15-18, 24, 27-28, 31, 35, 63-64, 70-71, 80-83
Ilanth, 13
Institute, 21, 35, 43, 51, 59, 83
Isle of Peril, 89
Iszic, 46
Iucounu the Laughing Magician, 63, 69, 87
Jack Vance (critical work), 21
James, Maister, 93
Jantiff (J. Ravensroke), 19, 39, 73, 75
Jung, Carl, 31ff.
Jupiter Award, 10-11, 89
Ka, 28, 82
Kahei, 28, 41, 82
Khors, 13, 32-33
Killing Machine, The, 12, 21, 68, 72, 76-77
Kotons, 31-32
Kruthe, 13, 58
Languages of Pao, The, 50-51, 57, 86
Larque, Lens, 32, 48, 62, 64, 77-78
Last Castle, The, 10, 34, 39-40, 43, 74, 91
Left Hand of Darkness, The, 23-24
Le Guin, Ursula K., 23, 96
Lekthwa, 41
Life, 16-17, 56

Lokhars, 13
Lucas, George, 21
Lyonesse, 86-89, 93-94
Maastricht, 33, 43
MacBeth, 38, 79-80
Maddoc, Uther, 39
Malagate the Woe, 48, 62, 64
Marmaduke, 28-29, 74
Marune: Alastor 993, 32-33, 45, 70, 72, 75, 78
Maske: Thaery, 45, 47, 73-75, 79
"Men Return, The," 19, 27, 35, 83-84, 86
Methlens, 77-78
"Miracle Workers, The," 35, 39, 86, 94
Moon Is a Harsh Mistress, The, 21, 24
"Moon Moth, The," 19, 38
Morningswake, 47
Mornune, 79-80
Mother of the Gods, 25
Murktime, 33
Museum of Man, 78
Navarth, 17, 22, 92
"New Prime, The," 19, 34, 68, 96
"Nightfall," 15
Odysseus and *Odyssey*, 46, 87
Oliphane, 41
Onmale, 31
Organisms, 83-84
Palace of Love, The, 17-18, 58, 68, 77, 92
Palesedrans, 81
Pao, 34
Patasz, Zhde, 46
Pharesm the Sorcerer, 19, 31
Phung, 13
Pnume and Pnumekin, 12-13, 20, 22, 28, 33, 47, 62
Pnume, The, 20, 53, 59, 61-62
Prime Directive, 27
prutanshyr, 65
Rampole, Robin, 64-65
Reith, Adam, 12, 15, 17, 20, 25-28, 31, 33, 38, 46-47, 56, 62-64, 67, 69-70, 75
Retief, 73, 96
Rhialto the Marvellous, 86-87
Rhunes, 23, 32, 54
Rianlle, Kaiark of Eccord, 45
Ridolph, Magnus, 10, 37, 67, 90
Rogushkoi, 14, 18, 80-83
Rolus, Arwin, 71
Sacerdotes, 30, 56
"Sail 25," 90, 96
Sailmaker Beach, 13, 72
Sajarano, 63, 80-83
Salazar, Sam, 35

Saltations to Finuka, 25
Sanduskers, 13
Sarkovy, 16, 27-29, 62
Scott, Ridley, 18
Servants of the Wankh, 15-16, 25-26, 37, 45-46, 52
Sharah, Aun, 81
Shillinsk, 15, 17
Shker, 14
Showboat World, 37-38, 68, 74, 79-80, 89
Silverberg, Robert, 64
Sirenese, 19, 41
Sivishe, 42
Slaves of the Klau, 13, 27, 29, 31
Smade of Smade's Planet, 50
Smith, Joe, 26, 30-31
Son of the Tree, 26, 30, 37, 74
Song of the Ka, 30-31, 47, 83, 94
Space Opera, 37, 68, 89
Star King, The, 10, 16, 46, 68, 74, 76
Star Trek, 27
Sturgeon, Theodore, 49
Suldrun, Princess, 87, 93
Suserane, 18
Tarvoke, Ghyl, 26, 39-40, 43, 47, 71, 75, 79
Thangs, 13
Theurgic cult, 25
Thissell, Edwer, 38
Tiedman, Richard, 61
Tintle's Shade, 73
Tinzy, Jheral, 48
To Live Forever, 22, 34, 39, 54, 74, 89
Tolkien, J. R. R., 87, 93
Tom Jones, 69
Traz, 33-34, 64, 69-70
Tree, The, 30-31
Treesong, Howard Alan, 35-36, 48, 62, 78, 95
Trevanyi, 74
Trullion: Alastor 2262, 33, 45, 64, 73-75, 86
Trumble, Sion, 77
Tschai series, 10, 12, 20, 27, 31, 37, 46-47, 56, 67-70
Wael, 45, 79
Wankh and Wankhmen, 12-13, 70
Weird Tales, 91
Whispers, 73
Windle, Billy, 72
Woudiver, Aila, 63
Wyst: Alastor 1716, 34, 43, 71, 73, 75
Yao, 13, 33
Ymph, Ramus, 45, 73, 79
Yob the Fish God, 24-25
Zaccare, 14, 33, 41
Zamp, Apollon, 15, 19, 37-38, 45, 57, 79-80

www.ingramcontent.com/pod-product-compliance
Lightning Source LLC
LaVergne TN
LVHW041633070426
835507LV00008B/592